NONPROFIT MANAGEMENT EDUCATION

NONPROFIT MANAGEMENT EDUCATION

U.S. and World Perspectives

Edited by Michael O'Neill
Kathleen Fletcher

PRAEGER

Westport, Connecticut
London

Library of Congress Cataloging-in-Publication Data

Nonprofit management education : U.S. and world perspectives / edited
   by Michael O'Neill, Kathleen Fletcher.
      p.   cm.
   Includes bibliographical references and index.
   ISBN 0–275–96115–X (alk. paper)
      1. Nonprofit organizations—Management—Study and teaching
   (Higher)   2. Nonprofit organizations—Management—Study and teaching
   (Higher)—United States.   I. O'Neill, Michael, 1938–   .
   II. Fletcher, Kathleen.
   HD62.6.N664   1998
   658′.048′071173—dc21   98–14904

British Library Cataloguing in Publication Data is available.

Library of Congress Catalog Card Number: 98–14904
ISBN: 0–275–96115–X

First published in 1998

Praeger Publishers, 88 Post Road West, Westport, CT 06881
An imprint of Greenwood Publishing Group, Inc.

Printed in the United States of America

The paper used in this book complies with the
Permanent Paper Standard issued by the National
Information Standards Organization (Z39.48–1984).

10 9 8 7 6 5 4 3 2 1

Contents

PART 2 SPECIAL ISSUES

PART 3 THEORETICAL ISSUES

Illustrations

FIGURE

Preface

This book grew out of a March 1996 conference hosted by the University of San Francisco's Institute for Nonprofit Organization Management. The conference drew 125 educators, scholars, and practitioners from 14 nations. A similar but smaller conference in 1986 produced the book *Educating Managers for Nonprofit Organizations* (O'Neill and Young, 1988), which has been widely used in the formulation of such programs. The present book is offered as a further guide to the central issues of this still new field of higher education.

Between the 1986 and 1996 conferences, there had been a proliferation of individual courses, concentrations in various graduate degree programs, and self-standing master's degrees in nonprofit management. The earlier conference, which took place when the field was just beginning, included representatives only from the United States, England, and Canada. The 1996 conference made it clear that nonprofit management education had not only grown rapidly in the United States but also spread to many other countries.

Ten of the 35 papers presented at the 1996 conference are included in this book, along with an introductory chapter on the history, current issues, and future of nonprofit management education. Several groups will benefit from reading this book. Practitioners will learn more about the opportunities available for professional study. Educators will find models of programs and discussion of important curricular, faculty, and administrative issues. Scholars will find research and theory on this new field of higher education. All readers will find a valuable introduction to the central issues and opportunities of nonprofit management education.

Following Chapter 1, the book is divided into three parts, with chapters on national case studies, key issues in nonprofit management education, and theoretical concerns. In Chapter 2, Naomi B. Wish and Roseanne M. Mirabella report on a survey of nonprofit management education programs in the United States. Mark Lyons reports on the Australian scene in Chapter 3. Chris Cornforth, Rob Paton, and Julian Batsleer discuss in Chapter 4 a distance education program in the United Kingdom. In Chapter 5, Gemma Donnelly-Cox and Geoffrey MacKechnie describe an emerging program in Ireland.

Chapters 6 through 9 focus on several major issues in the field. In Chapter 6, Mary Tschirhart reports on a study of what different stakeholders want from nonprofit education programs. Norman A. Dolch, Roland Kidwell, Jr., Jeffrey Sadow, and Jimmie Smith, in Chapter 7, turn to nonprofit management education on the undergraduate level, presenting four different models used by the American Humanics program. In Chapter 8, Jeffrey L. Brudney and Gretchen E. Stringer document the relative absence of the topic of volunteer management from nonprofit education programs and ask why coverage of this important area is so limited. Rick Smith, in Chapter 9, examines the role that management support organizations have played or could play in the development and operation of university-based nonprofit management programs.

Important theoretical issues are presented in Chapters 10 and 11. Dennis R. Young uses the game analogy in Chapter 10 to discuss the ways in which university politics may affect nonprofit management education programs. Lester M. Salamon, in Chapter 11, suggests that nonprofit management education may be the right answer to the wrong question and argues that education should focus on developing "public citizens" with the knowledge and skills to manage the relationships between the governmental and nonprofit sectors.

The history of higher education shows all too clearly that some promising ideas come and go, while others take root and thrive. This book documents the growth of the nonprofit management education idea and addresses some of the key issues that will determine its future.

The W. K. Kellogg Foundation, the leading funder of nonprofit management education efforts, provided financial support for this conference-book project.

NONPROFIT MANAGEMENT EDUCATION

1

Nonprofit Management Education: History, Current Issues, and the Future

Michael O'Neill

INTRODUCTION

The first university-based generic nonprofit management education (NME) programs date from the early 1980s in the United States and a few other countries. As Naomi B. Wish and Roseanne M. Mirabella document in Chapter 2 of this book, there are now more than 70 such programs in the United States alone. The number of these programs has been doubling every three or four years. Several hundred students enroll in such programs annually. Chapters 3, 4, and 5 document similar efforts in Australia, Ireland, and England.

In spite of such rapid growth, NME still faces the same questions it has faced for nearly two decades: Should it exist at all? Should it be part of a master of business administration (MBA) degree, a master of public administration (MPA) degree, or an industry-based degree like arts administration; or should it be a free-standing degree dedicated totally to nonprofit management? Who should teach in such programs? What kinds of students should be targeted? What should the curriculum be? How can such programs gain institutional support and academic acceptance? In a field that has focused almost exclusively on the master's level, should there be more doctoral and undergraduate programs? Should there be not only programs but also departments and even schools of nonprofit management?

This book is intended to assist interested parties in developing answers to such questions.

WHY NONPROFIT MANAGEMENT EDUCATION?

Management or administration is simply defined as "getting things done through other people." Countless such activities, from organizing a high school reunion to running a grocery store, take place without apparent need of formal management education. A few types of management activity, typically those involving many people, programs, and resources over long periods of time, have led to the creation of formal management education, usually focused on large business and government organizations. The recent addition of NME raises legitimate questions about the rationale or need for this new field. One might argue that all management is basically the same and therefore that nonprofit managers should take MBA and other time-tested management degrees. Or one might argue, as Lester M. Salamon does in Chapter 11, that the interdependence of nonprofit and government work calls for a new type of "border management" skills and preparation. Or one might contend that nonprofits have fared well so far without the cumbersome formalities of formal management education and therefore should continue unencumbered.

The development of nonprofit management education has been based on the theory that there are significant differences in (1) the organizational reality of nonprofits, as distinguished from for-profit and government entities, and therefore in (2) the knowledge, skills, attitudes, and values needed to manage nonprofits. Following are the chief differences alleged to exist between nonprofits and other kinds of organizations (O'Neill and Young, 1988, pp. 3–8; Mason, 1984, pp. 20–22 and generally; Billis and Harris, 1996).

Purpose/Mission

The fundamental purpose of a business organization is to make money. The immediate task may be to make computers or provide life insurance, but the overriding purpose is to make a profit. For a nonprofit, by contrast, making money is subsidiary to the overriding purpose of providing some good or service. An unprofitable product will be changed or discarded by a business, whereas many nonprofit services barely break even and some, like opera and private education, are operated continuously at a deficit (Bowen and Baumol, 1968; Levy, 1986). In a business, goods and services have instrumental or secondary value; the primary value is making money. In a nonprofit, the service is the primary value; making money is a means to that end. "It is a matter of direction. One generates the money in order to do the job. The other does the job in order to generate the money" (Mason, 1984, p. 88).

Values

Many nonprofits are strongly value-oriented. Examples include religious organizations, most nonprofit schools and colleges, and many advocacy organizations. All organizations have institutional values, but in for-profits the values are likely to be subordinate to the profit orientation—product quality, honesty with customers, and the like—whereas in many nonprofits the values are central to the mission of the organization.

Resource Acquisition

Nonprofits, like all organizations, must acquire resources, including money. In a business, money typically comes directly from the sale of goods and services. Thus, while marketing/sales strategies may be elaborate and expensive, the basic structure of the resource acquisition task is fairly simple. Government resource acquisition is somewhat more complex, but the great bulk of revenue comes from taxation; at least as important for present purposes is the fact that most government agencies are not directly involved in revenue acquisition. By contrast, nonprofits receive their money from several different source types: consumers of the organizations' goods and services, government grants and contracts, donations from individuals, grants from foundations and corporations, interest on endowment and other funds, and subsidiary for-profit enterprises. Resource acquisition in nonprofits is thus a more complex management task, calling for a greater variety of skills and knowledge. "No other sector seems to put such diverse demands on managers to maintain organizational sources of sustenance and growth" (O'Neill and Young, 1988, p. 6).

Bottom Line

A related argument is that nonprofits do not have the same clarity regarding acceptable performance that is provided by the market for business firms and by the election system for political/governmental groups. A nonprofit therefore must be managed without the benefit of clear bottom-line performance indicators and must persuade funders, trustees, and clients that the agency's efforts are effective and efficient.

Legal Context

While all organizations have legal constraints and privileges, nonprofits are legally different in significant ways from for-profit and government entities. For example, nonprofits are prohibited from distributing financial surpluses to their principal "shareholders"—members, volunteers, and staff. Such profit distribution is the very purpose of a for-profit firm. Nonprofits are exempted from paying corporate income tax, property tax, and in some states and localities sales tax. Charitable nonprofits may receive tax-deductible contributions. Nonprofits are prohibited from engaging in certain types of political activity. These and other legal differences present unique challenges and opportunities for nonprofit managers.

Worker Characteristics

In many nonprofit organizations, most of the workers are unpaid volunteers. The absence of payment removes a major incentive that is present in business and government organizations. Further, the nondistribution constraint eliminates most forms of direct profit-sharing for paid staff. Demographic differences are also relevant. Largely because of the industries they are in (health care, education, social work, arts and culture, and so forth), nonprofit employees are more educated and more likely to be professionals than for-profit workers. Nonprofit workers, paid and unpaid, are much more likely to be female than for-profit workers (Odendahl and O'Neill, 1994). If management is "getting things done through other people," worker characteristics will significantly shape effective management practices.

Governance

Nonprofits are governed by boards made up of volunteers who come from the community, act as trustees for the public interest, and may not benefit from the agencies' net revenue. Drucker (1989) has argued that governing boards play a uniquely important role in nonprofit organizations. A study by Herman and Heimovics (1991) suggests that "board-regarding behavior" is critically important for nonprofit managers. While there are great varieties in board roles in all three types of organizations, nonprofit managers typically need and have closer working relationships with their boards than is the case in business and government agencies.

Organizational Complexity

Nonprofits frequently offer several different kinds of service, serve multiple constituencies, depend on a half dozen or more different types of funding sources, and have different kinds of workers. Mason (1984, pp. 171–179) argues that nonprofit organizations are typically more complex than business organizations, giving as an example a federation of churches in a metropolitan area "with only 20 employees. Yet it operates over 50 different projects, utilizing 2,000 volunteers, touching such aspects of community life as education, health, family life, communications, public welfare, and politics. It involves all aspects of the city from the illiterate poor to the country club power brokers" (p. 172).

Several points should be made about these postulated differences between nonprofits and other organizations:

1. Some nonprofits, such as research agencies and hospitals, are much more like their for-profit counterparts than are nonprofits such as churches and advocacy organizations. More generally, many nonprofits are adopting "business-like" strategies in areas like marketing and sales.
2. Other nonprofits, such as educational and social service groups, are more similar to their government counterparts and often have few for-profit counterparts.
3. There is significant commonality in all forms of management. Separate NME programs may be justified by the organizational differences sketched above, but it would be unwise, and a disservice to students, to emphasize nonprofit uniqueness to the point of understating this commonality. A related pragmatic consideration is that much of our knowledge about management and organizations has come from the study of business firms and is located in business schools and publications.
4. While intrinsic considerations should dominate the debate about NME, it is important to recognize the influence of extrinsic factors such as academic traditions, politics, and incentive systems. Such factors may help explain business schools' relative lack of interest in the education of nonprofit managers. It may be that business schools, consistent with for-profit culture, have not seen it in their best interests to pursue NME, independent of any intrinsic merits of the NME case. This, however, may change if NME continues to demonstrate the viability of this new market.

HISTORICAL DEVELOPMENT

Although the management of complex enterprises such as cities, building projects, wars, large-scale trade, and religious and secular organizations has been evident for thousands of years, formal management education is little more than a century old. In the late nineteenth century, programs were developed at the University of Pennsylvania (Wharton), the University of California, Harvard University, and other institutions of higher education. Given the dominance at that time of large for-profit firms, these programs not surprisingly focused on business education and gave little attention to the management of government or nonprofit enterprises. It is worth noting that this still dominant form of management education is largely a historical accident. If management education had developed during the times of the Egyptian pharaohs or Roman emperors, it would have been "public" administration. If management education had developed during the time of the medieval popes or caliphs, it would have been "religious" administration.

As nonbusiness enterprises grew, management education programs were developed for government, education, health, social work, arts, and other types of administration. Business education, however, remained and still remains the dominant form, reflecting the dominant role of business in American and most other societies.

Nonprofit management education in the United States developed largely in response to the rapid growth of what is now called the nonprofit sector during the half-century following World War II, and especially during the three decades since the mid 1960s. Nonreligious charitable nonprofits grew from 27,500 in 1946 (Hall, 1994, p. 31) and 138,000 in 1969 (Weisbrod, 1988, p. 169) to 650,000 in 1996 (U.S. Internal Revenue Service, 1996). For at least ten years before the mid 1960s, about 5,000 new nonprofits of all types were approved each year by the IRS; during the last two decades, 40,000 have been approved annually (Weisbrod, 1988, p. 170; and subsequent IRS annual reports). In recent decades, the nonprofit sector has grown much faster than the business and government sectors (although these comparative growth rates are somewhat deceptive since nonprofits began from such a small base). According to an IRS report, "Between 1975 and 1990, assets of tax-exempt organizations increased in real terms by over 150 percent while revenues increased by over 227 percent. This is in comparison to a growth in [U.S.] real GDP of 52 percent over the same period" (Skelly, 1994, p. 556). The American nonprofit sector currently consists of 1.5 million organizations, 10 million paid staff, 90 million volunteers, and annual revenue of $600 billion (Hodgkinson, Weitzman, Abrahams, Crutchfield, and Stevenson, 1996, pp. 3, 13, 140).

In the late 1970s and early 1980s, several universities began creating programs to tap this new market. In 1977, Columbia University established an Institute for Not-for-Profit Management, which inaugurated a certificate program for nonprofit managers. The University of Missouri at Kansas City launched a nonprofit management concentration within its MPA degree in 1981. The University of San Francisco began a similar concentration in 1983; two years later it became the nation's first free-standing master of nonprofit administration program. George Washington University started a master of association management degree in 1984; this unique program (since closed) was aimed primarily at managers of nonprofit trade and professional associations in the nation's capital. The University of Colorado at Denver created both master's and doctoral nonprofit management concentrations within their public administration degrees in the early 1980s. In

1986, the New School for Social Research converted its master of professional studies in fundraising management, which started in 1979, to a master of science in nonprofit management. The State University of New York at Stony Brook created a nonprofit management concentration in 1986. Case Western Reserve University began its master of nonprofit organizations program in 1989, having fielded a nonprofit management certificate program in 1988.

There were parallel developments in other nations. In Canada, York University in Toronto inaugurated a voluntary-sector management concentration in its MBA program in 1983. In 1984, England's Brunel University began a voluntary-sector concentration area in its master of arts in public and social administration. This program was later transferred to the London School of Economics and Political Science, which created a master of science in voluntary-sector organization in 1987. Australia's University of Technology at Sydney began a master of management in community management in 1991; an associate diploma in community organizations had been inaugurated by the same institution in 1986. There are now similar programs in Sweden, Italy, New Zealand, Switzerland, and Argentina.

In addition to full degree programs or concentrations, a number of universities began to offer individual courses on nonprofit management, typically electives in MPA, MBA, master of social work (MSW), or other programs. An April 1997 survey by the University of San Francisco identified 433 courses in more than 100 universities.

While most of the program development was at the master's level, there were some efforts at other levels. As indicated above, the University of Colorado at Denver initiated a doctoral concentration (since terminated) in the early 1980s. The Union Institute for Experimenting Colleges and Universities started a nonresidential doctoral program titled "Program in Philanthropy and Leadership" in 1985. On the undergraduate level, the American Humanics Institute contracted with several universities to offer administrative programs for students interested in youth service administration. In Chapter 7 of this book, Norman A. Dolch, Roland Kidwell, Jr., Jeffrey Sadow, and Jimmie Smith report on American Humanics programs at four universities. Indiana University's business school inaugurated an undergraduate major in nonprofit administration in 1995. Several universities began to offer nonprofit management certificate programs; a 1997 survey listed 49 nonprofit certificate programs in the United States and one each in Canada, Australia, and England (Koziol, 1997).

It is important to note the training context within which these university education programs developed. As Rick Smith points out in Chapter 9, nonprofit training and technical assistance agencies, now generally known as management support organizations (MSOs), have long played an important role in improving nonprofit management. MSOs like the Support Centers and the Fund Raising School currently train more than 50,000 nonprofit managers a year in short-term (three hours to one week) workshops and seminars. In some cases, MSOs have helped shape university NME programs through community advisory boards and other such mechanisms.

Another contextual factor has been the growth of nonprofit research centers, journals, professional magazines, and book publishing. Yale University's Program on Non-Profit Organizations was founded in 1977 and has produced more than 200 working papers, dozens of articles, and several books. Nonprofit research centers have also been established at Boston College, the City University of New York, Duke University, the New York University School of Law, and the Queensland University of Technology in Brisbane, Australia. Additionally, some of the institutions that offer educational programs, such as Johns Hopkins University, Indiana University, Case Western Reserve University, the London School of Economics, the University of San Francisco, the University of Missouri-Kansas City, and the University of Technology at Sydney also have active research programs. The 1980s and 1990s have seen an explosion of publications about voluntary, nonprofit, and philanthropic issues. Jossey-Bass Publishers, the Foundation Center, Oxford University Press, Indiana University Press, Yale University Press, Johns Hopkins University Press, John Wiley Company, and other book publishers have developed nonprofit series. Three scholarly journals, *Nonprofit Management and Leadership, Voluntas*, and *Nonprofit and Voluntary Sector Quarterly* (formerly the *Journal of Voluntary Action Research*), serve the field; and there are several professional journals and newspapers, such as *Advancing Philanthropy, Foundation News and Commentary*, and the *Chronicle of Philanthropy*. Scholarly groups include the Association for Research on Nonprofit Organizations and Voluntary Action, the International Society for Third-Sector Research, and the Australian and New Zealand Third Sector Research Society. Other scholarly and professional associations such as the National Association of Schools of Public Affairs and Administration (NASPAA) and the Academy of Management include special interest groups on nonprofit issues. Independent Sector, a U.S. coalition of national nonprofit organizations and foundations, has actively supported the growth of nonprofit research and management education. The Aspen Institute's Nonprofit Sector Research Fund has supported several dozen projects.

Growth in the number of university programs inspired the formation of the Nonprofit Academic Centers Council (NACC), whose purpose is to increase communication and collaboration among university-based centers for nonprofit studies. This group sponsors, among other projects, a scholarship program for students of color seeking NME degrees.

Foundation, corporate, and individual financial support has played an influential role in the development of NME. The W. K. Kellogg Foundation alone has made grants totaling more than $20 million in support of NME and related efforts. The Lilly Endowment, Inc., has given more than $25 million to Indiana University's Center on Philanthropy in support of a variety of projects, including NME. John C. Whitehead donated $10 million to Harvard Business School for support of nonprofit management programs. Gus and Rita Hauser have recently given Harvard's Kennedy School of Public Affairs $10 million to establish the Hauser Center for Nonprofit Institutions. The Mandel family in Cleveland has given more than $4 million to Case Western Reserve University in support of its Mandel Center for Nonprofit Organizations, which has also received substantial funding from other sources. The University of San Francisco's Institute for Nonprofit Organization Management has received more than $5 million from 40 foundations and corporations in support of work in NME and related projects.

CURRENT ISSUES, FUTURE CHALLENGES

Like organizations, social movements, and individuals, new academic and professional fields go through stages of development. Nonprofit management education is no longer a new, untested idea. About 100 universities around the world have established such programs, and several thousand students have enrolled. However, NME is far from a mature, established field. The following are some of the chief issues, questions, problems, opportunities, and challenges that this new field faces now and during the next decade or two.

Institutionalization

As Dennis R. Young points out in Chapter 10, university politics is a serious, complex, and high-stakes game. New academic programs must compete with much more established programs for faculty positions, student financial aid, support staff and services, and attention and support from department chairs, deans, provosts, presidents, and trustees. Academic leadership, student response, and external funding have played important roles in the creation and initial success of NME programs. Long-term success will depend on NME's ability not only to maintain and increase current course offerings, enrollment, and administrative support but also to secure tenure-track faculty positions dedicated to this effort. Full-time faculty interest and involvement is essential to the stabilization of NME. Dedicated faculty positions and endowed chairs represent a critically important next step for the institutionalization of NME.

Academic Acceptance

Institutionalization will depend largely on the decisions of individual universities. These influence and are influenced by the acceptance and credibility of NME within academia generally. Presentations at academic and professional conferences, peer-reviewed articles and books, citations by other scholars, grants, and academic honors are all necessary for the increasing credibility of this field. Academic acceptance is partly a function of the development of a distinct body of knowledge and theoretical base, some of which, with respect to NME and nonprofit/philanthropic studies generally, has emerged during the past decade within and among various academic disciplines.

Academic Base

Since the field began, there has been continuous discussion as to what is the most appropriate academic base for NME. While there seems to be no more consensus on this issue than there was at a 1986 conference on NME (see chapters by Levy, Cyert, DiMaggio, and Slavin in O'Neill and Young, 1988), it has become clear that the numerically dominant model is the MPA concentration in nonprofit management. As Wish and Mirabella report in Chapter 2, more than half the programs in the United States follow this model. There are still very few MBA concentrations in NME. There may be a greater commonality of interest, values, knowledge, and skills between public administration and nonprofit administration, and business schools may not see NME as in their own interests. An interesting case study will be that of Harvard University, where both the Business School and the Kennedy School of Public Affairs have recently received more than $10 million to strengthen nonprofit institutions.

In addition to the MPA and MBA models, several institutions, including the University of San Francisco, Case Western Reserve University, the New School for Social Research, Regis University, and the London School of Economics, have free-standing NME programs. Like MBA and MPA programs, free-standing NME programs are separate and focused solely on one sector, with courses, students, and faculty from that sector.

Industry-based programs are still common. These include programs in social work administration, arts administration, health care administration, private school administration, and the like. Mark Lyons points out in Chapter 3 that, in Australia, far more nonprofit managers are trained in industry-based than in generic management programs. Slavin (1988) argued that some professions, like health care or social work, tend to reject managers who are not steeped in the culture of those professions.

The particular academic base of NME programs probably matters less than the quality of and institutional support for the programs. Therefore the choice of an MPA, MBA, MSW, independent, industry-based, or other model should be made only after careful analysis of institutional support factors, including faculty strength.

Accreditation

Since the great majority of NME programs are MPA or MBA concentrations, both of which degrees have national accreditation bodies, the question of accreditation applies principally to independent programs. There has been no move in this direction, almost certainly because of the newness of the field and the small number of such programs. However, there is merit in the idea of exploring some sort of external review process, perhaps in collaboration with NASPAA, the association that accredits MPA programs.

Doctoral, Undergraduate, and Certificate Programs

Most of the NME programs developed during the last 20 years have been at the master's degree level. The next 10 to 20 years should see more attention to doctoral, undergraduate, and certificate programs. There are currently about 50 university-based nonprofit certificate programs, with widely different academic requirements and relationships to degree programs. Certificates provide a useful way for universities to (1) assess student interest in NME, leading in some cases to the development of degree programs or concentrations; (2) meet the needs of students who do not want or need a master's degree; and (3) provide quality NME without the time and expense of degree work.

Undergraduate management education programs present unique opportunities and challenges. Programs for traditional (age 18–22) undergraduates would need not only to create curriculum and generate faculty and administrative support but also to develop nonprofit career awareness in potential students. Another question, debated in management education circles generally, is the utility of management education for younger students. Degree-completion NME programs for "nontraditional" (age 25+) undergraduates represent another possible development.

The doctoral level presents other opportunities and challenges. Leduc and McAdam suggested at the 1986 conference that, while the main emphasis should be placed on the master's level, there was a role for doctoral work: "The doctoral level presents an opportunity to train researchers and policy analysts as well as a few scholars who could fill the teaching and research positions necessary to offer the master's level programs" (Leduc and McAdam, 1988, p. 98; see also O'Neill and Young, 1988, p. 19). The almost total absence of NME on the doctoral level may have several causes: (1) This is a new scholarly and teaching field; some would question whether there is at this point an adequate intellectual base for a doctoral program. (2) There are so few NME faculty positions that there is little or no demand of that type for NME doctoral graduates; however, there is increasing demand for faculty part of whose responsibility is to teach NME courses. (3) Doctoral programs require significantly more time, effort, faculty resources, and library resources per student than master's programs. In spite of these inhibitors, the growth of the NME field makes it likely that the next 10 to 20 years will see more activity on the doctoral level, from individual course electives to a few concentrations.

Curriculum

The curricular content of NME is to a large degree shaped by the academic base and level of the programs. MPA- and MBA-based programs are heavily influenced by accreditation requirements and academic traditions in those fields. Doctoral, master's, undergraduate, and professional certificate programs will have different curricula because of the differing experiential and academic backgrounds of the students. Other curricular influences include the age and administrative experience of the students, the academic interests and strengths of the host institutions, and local community needs. In Chapter 6, Mary Tschirhart explores the curricular priorities of three interested groups: nonprofit managers, faculty who teach in NME programs, and students or prospective students in NME programs. In spite of all these differentiating forces, an examination of current nonprofit management curricula reveals a considerable degree of similarity. Nearly all programs offer course work in financial management, fundraising, marketing, and introduction to nonprofit issues. Other common courses are human resource management, governance, planning, ethics, law, information management, and management/organization theory. Jeffrey L. Brudney and Gretchen E. Stringer point out in Chapter 8 that volunteer administration is largely neglected in NME curricula, in spite of the extensive presence of volunteers in nonprofit organizations.

Students and Graduates

While there is no systematic, cross-program study of the characteristics of NME students, anecdotal evidence suggests that the great majority of students are in their late 20s, 30s, and 40s, with several years of work and some administrative experience in nonprofit organizations. Most students are employed by social service agencies; other fields represented include arts, religious, education, health, advocacy, and funding agencies. Most students work full- or part-time while enrolled in NME programs. Women constitute the majority of NME students, in some programs reaching 75 percent of total enrollment. Students of color seem underrepresented; NACC has initiated a national scholarship program to attract more minority students into nonprofit management master's degrees, and some universities have sponsored similar scholarship efforts. Nonprofit management students have undergraduate majors primarily in the social sciences and humanities; there are few business, math, engineering, or physical sciences majors. There are no generally available data on the academic performance of these students, as measured by former and current grades, GRE or GMAT scores, or the like. Nor are there any published studies tracking the graduates of such programs.

The fact that so many students have enrolled in this new degree area is one of the most important and least studied aspects of the NME phenomenon. There is great need for research on the demographic characteristics, academic backgrounds, current and past work experience, and aspirations of these students, as well as their assessment of the quality and relevance of NME programs.

Faculty

Since most NME programs are concentrations within an MPA, MBA, or other degree, the faculty experienced by nonprofit students are primarily full-time faculty trained in disciplines relevant to public and business administration. Virtually all NME programs use some adjunct faculty, usually practitioners who work full time as nonprofit executive directors, fundraisers, financial managers, lawyers, consultants, and the like. A general conclusion of the 1986 conference was, "Nonprofit management programs should follow the experience of the best professional education programs in combining theory and research with practice, and in including both full-time research-oriented faculty and part-time practitioner faculty in the program delivery" (O'Neill and Young, 1988, p. 21), and that recommendation seems still honored in practice. There is considerable variation, however, in the mix of full- and part-time faculty from one program to another. If one looks only at freestanding programs and the nonprofit courses in MPA and MBA concentrations, the percentage of courses taught by adjunct faculty seems to range between 10 percent and 75 percent at various institutions.

Faculty academic background is highly diverse, because of the newness of the NME field, the high percentage of adjunct faculty, and the interdisciplinary nature of not only NME but also some of the "parent disciplines" of business and public administration. Degrees commonly represented among NME faculty are public administration, business administration, social work, political science, economics, sociology, education, and history.

Funding

Both university support and external funding have played a major role in the development of this new academic field. About $60 million has been contributed to NME and related work (research, conferences, publications, and so forth) by foundations, corporations, and individuals. Most of this money has gone to a relatively few institutions, including Indiana University, Harvard University, Case Western Reserve University, Johns Hopkins University, the University of Missouri-Kansas City, and the University of San Francisco. The need for both university support and external funding continues to grow. Outside Harvard, only two institutions have NME endowed chairs, and those are heavily administrative in orientation. The number of dedicated faculty positions is very low. At most institutions, student financial assistance is sparse. More money is needed to develop cases and other teaching materials and to support new instructional technologies such as distance learning (see the remarks of Chris Cornforth, Rob Paton, and Julian Batsleer in Chapter 4 on NME distance learning). Although established fields receive more money than new fields, NME has at least one advantage: the high percentage of its students, graduates, faculty, and advisory board members who could lend fundraising expertise.

Departments and Schools

It is not too early to raise the question of whether there should be departments and schools of nonprofit management. As indicated earlier, the fact that there are departments and schools of business and public (government) administration is largely a historical accident related to the number and size of those types of organizations. The growth of the nonprofit sector makes it reasonable to pose the department/school question about NME. Ideally, all management education at a university should be located within one school of management, with general course work and some separate courses and field experiences for students interested in business, government, and nonprofits in health care, education, social work, the arts, religion, and the like. There is little if any evidence to date that such ideal visions can survive the powerful traditions and faculty incentives of the established academic fields, especially business administration. The efforts of institutions such as Yale and UCLA to develop inclusive schools of management have largely failed: these are essentially business schools by another name. Nonprofit management education, for reasons of survival, growth, and quality, must sooner or later face the question of whether to develop departments, schools, doctoral programs, tenured faculty positions, and other academic trappings that characterize stable professional education programs.

The following chapters detail some of the varieties, contributions, problems, and accomplishments of NME. The last 15–20 years have seen pioneering work, rapid expansion, and the field-testing of several models of NME. The next 15–20 years should be marked by more aggressive efforts to gain institutional and external support, build academic credibility, secure student financial aid, develop program offerings at several levels and in several instructional formats, strengthen the full-time tenure-track faculty base, and move toward broad accreditation standards. The editors hope that this book and its 1988 companion volume will enlighten and shape this still very new and evolving field.

Part 1

National Case Studies

2

Nonprofit Management Education: Current Offerings and Practices in University-Based Programs

Naomi B. Wish and Roseanne M. Mirabella

INTRODUCTION

In 1990 Naomi Wish collected baseline data on universities and colleges offering graduate courses in the management of nonprofit organizations (Wish, 1991). To be included in her sample, programs had to be

- offered by a college or university rather than by a profit-making or nonprofit organization;
- oriented primarily toward management rather than policy or history;
- focused primarily on nonprofit organizations rather than on the public and private sectors;
- generic, rather than focusing on only one subgroup of nonprofit organizations (for example, health administration, arts administration, religious institution management).

Wish found that in 1990 only 17 universities offered a graduate concentration (three or more courses) in the management of nonprofit organizations. In a subsequent study in 1992, she found 32 universities with such programs (Wish, 1993). In related studies conducted by the Independent Sector, Hodgkinson (1988) and later Crowder and Hodgkinson (1991) collected information on academic centers and institutes focusing on the study of philanthropy, voluntarism, and nonprofit activity. They found that the number of academic centers had increased from 19 in 1988 to 26 in 1991. The growth in nonprofit management education has clearly been sudden and swift. Yet because of this rapid growth, it has been difficult to study systematically the number and types of educational programs and to consider their impact on the nonprofit sector.

In this chapter we report the results of the first part of a two-phase research project. In the current study, based on a survey of universities and colleges, we seek to answer the following questions: What is the current universe of graduate nonprofit management programs, as defined by Wish's five criteria? Where are these programs situated in the university—in colleges of arts and sciences, business, public administration, or elsewhere? What courses are offered? What degrees are granted? In the second phase of the study, which began in autumn 1996, we examine how these programs impact upon the nonprofit sector.

METHODOLOGY

In September 1995, we mailed a questionnaire about nonprofit offerings to more than 1,000 colleges and universities that belong to the American Assembly of Collegiate Schools of Business (AACSB), the National Association of Public Affairs and Administration (NASPAA), the Association for Research on Nonprofit Organizations and Voluntary Action (ARNOVA), the Council on Social Work Education (CSWE), and the Nonprofit Academic Centers Council (NACC).[1] We sent reminder postcards to the entire list several weeks after the initial mailing. Next, we faxed questionnaires to a select group of colleges and universities, known to have programs of this type, that had not yet responded to the mailing. In addition, we used e-mail to send a reminder to members of ARNOVA.

Of the 1,358 questionnaires mailed, 343 were returned, for an overall response rate of 25 percent (Table 2.1).[2] The response rate for the NASPAA-affiliated schools, 36 percent, was the highest; the rate was lowest (18 percent) for those on the AACSB list. The CSWE social work schools posted a 27 percent response rate. An additional 90 questionnaires were returned by respondents on the other mailing lists, including ARNOVA-affiliated institutions, NACC institutions, and additional institutions targeted for mailing because of their interest in nonprofit management education. Of the 343 responding institutions, 166 (48 percent) offered some course work in nonprofit management.

Table 2.1
Institutions Offering Nonprofit Management Education, by Mailing List

	Number and Percentage of Questionnaires Returned	Responding Institutions Offering Nonprofit Management Courses
AACSB (N = 746)	136 (18%)	42 (31%)
NASPAA (N = 228)	82 (36%)	53 (65%)
Other (N = 253)	90 (36%)	51 (57%)
Totals (N = 1,358)	343 (25%)	166 (48%)

SUMMARY OF RESULTS

Growth in the Nonprofit Management Education Field

Seventy-six universities and colleges now offer graduate degree programs with a concentration (three or more courses) in the management of nonprofit organizations (see Appendix 2.1 for a list of these institutions). An additional 43 universities offer one or two graduate courses, usually financial management and generic nonprofit management. Forty-seven institutions offer noncredit courses, continuing education unit (CEU) courses, or undergraduate courses.

Along with the rapid increase in the number of universities offering at least three graduate courses in nonprofit management, we found a substantial increase in the number of programs located at institutions of higher learning in the South and Midwest. Almost 40 percent of these programs are located in the Midwest; this region, rather than the Northeast, has become dominant in this area. Growth in the Midwest is probably due to external funding of these programs by the W. K. Kellogg Foundation and the Lilly Endowment, Inc.; growth in the South, however, is not immediately explained by such external support. Table 2.2 shows the number of universities by region and compares Wish's 1992 findings with the current findings.

Table 2.2
Graduate Programs in Nonprofit Management, by Region

	Number and Percentage of Programs, 1992 ($N = 32$)	Number and Percentage of Programs, 1995 ($N = 76$)
Northeast	12 (38%)	22 (29%)
Midwest	11 (34%)	29 (38%)
South	3 (9%)	11 (14%)
West	6 (19%)	14 (18%)

Although the regional distribution of programs has changed, the types of schools or colleges within the university that house the nonprofit management program remain almost the same as before. Table 2.3 displays our most recent data in comparison with the data from Wish's 1992 study. Twenty-one percent of the graduate nonprofit management programs are located in colleges of public administration, but the educational coupling of the public with the nonprofit sector is probably even stronger than suggested by that figure. Many graduate programs in public administration that offer concentrations in nonprofit management are located in colleges of arts and sciences, as represented by the additional 22 percent in that category in Table 2.3.

Increasingly, however, nonprofit management programs are being housed elsewhere in universities. About 43 percent of the programs are located in divisions such as schools of professional studies or schools of social work or are interdisciplinary. The program at Case Western Reserve University, for example, offers courses in the schools of management, applied social sciences, and law. Finally, about 7 percent of the graduate programs are housed in a business school, and another 7 percent in a school of business and public administration.

Table 2.3
School or College That Houses Graduate Programs

	Number and Percentage of Programs, 1992 ($N = 32$)	Number and Percentage of Programs, 1995 ($N = 76$)
Arts and sciences	9 (28%)	17 (22%)
Business schools	3 (9%)	5 (7%)
Business and public administration	3 (9%)	5 (7%)
Public affairs and administration	6 (19%)	16 (21%)
Other school or college	11 (34%)	33 (43%)

The data on the graduate degrees substantiate the close relationship between professional education for leaders in the public sector and in the nonprofit sector. Table 2.4 shows that almost half of the programs (47 percent) grant an MPA degree; approximately 75 percent of these programs are housed in colleges of arts and sciences or public affairs and administration. As mentioned above, fully 43 percent of universities house their nonprofit management programs elsewhere in the institution. Consistent with this finding is the fact that 45 percent of the degrees are not MBAs or MPAs. The programs offering an MS degree (11 percent) show no pattern in regard to location. Of the remaining 34 percent of the degrees offered, 14 percent are the MSW, 9 percent are the MA, and 11 percent are other degrees such as the master of nonprofit management. Approximately 8 percent of the nonprofit programs lead to an MBA degree. Most of these programs are housed in schools of business or schools of business and public administration.

Of the programs with a graduate concentration in nonprofit management education, 35 (46 percent) also offer a certificate program. Almost two-thirds of the certificates are in nonprofit management or nonprofit management and leadership. The remaining certificate programs focus on areas such as fundraising, philanthropic studies, and specific subtopics such as arts administration or Jewish communal studies.

Nonprofit Management Course Offerings

In this section, we focus on the curricular elements of the programs reporting that they offer graduate courses in nonprofit management. We categorize the programs into three groups by the number of nonprofit courses offered: from three to five, from six to nine, and ten or more.

Most of the colleges and universities offering three to five courses focusing on nonprofit management include one that is devoted to generic nonprofit management and another that is directed toward financial management. The third is usually human resource management. Public policy and information management are also offered, although much less often than human resource management. Most of these programs are located in colleges of arts and sciences or colleges of public affairs and administration, and more than half are included in MPA degree programs.

Table 2.4
Graduate Nonprofit Management Programs, by Degree Granted

	Number and Percentage of Programs, 1992 ($N = 32$)	Number and Percentage of Programs, 1995 ($N = 76$)
MPA/Policy/Public Affairs	17 (53%)	36 (47%)
MBA	4 (13%)	6 (8%)
MS	5 (16%)	8 (11%)
MA	0	7 (9%)
MSW	0	11 (14%)
Other degree	6 (19%)	8 (11%)

Twenty-six of the responding programs offer six to nine courses in nonprofit management. These programs also include courses in nonprofit management, resource management, and human resources. However, these programs list additional courses in governance, ethics, philanthropy, and legal issues. Fully two-thirds of these programs offer at least one course in policy or program analysis and evaluation. Once again, most of these programs are associated with the MPA degree.

Finally, 14 programs offer 10 or more courses in nonprofit management. Students can select from an impressive array of courses such as "Orchestrating the Capital Campaign" and "Cross-Cultural Dimensions of Philanthropy," allowing students to specialize in a particular aspect of nonprofit management. For example, Case Western Reserve University offers at least four courses that focus on fundraising and development.

In some of the programs with more than 10 courses, students take all of their graduate credits in courses focused on the management of nonprofit organizations. For example, for the master of nonprofit administration degree offered through the University of San Francisco's College of Professional Studies, students complete 36 units in the management of nonprofit organizations. Seattle University's executive master of not-for-profit leadership program requires students to take 10 courses in nonprofit management. Students progress through both these programs in cohort groups.

Other programs, such as those at the New School for Social Research and Regis University, have a small generic core of courses with all electives in the management of nonprofit organizations.

Table 2.5
Services Provided to Nonprofit Community by Nonprofit Management Programs

Services	Number and Percentage of Programs Providing Other Services ($N = 76$)
Internships	60 (79%)
Technical Assistance	46 (61%)
Workshops	39 (51%)
Conferences	38 (50%)
Newsletters	24 (32%)

About half of the programs offering 10 or more courses offer the MPA degree, while the other half offer a master of nonprofit management or philanthropic studies.

These 76 graduate degree programs with three or more courses in nonprofit management usually reach out to the nonprofit sector and its community-based groups through a host of other activities. The data in Table 2.5 demonstrate that most of the programs place interns, give technical assistance, sponsor conferences, and conduct workshops. Programs with three or more courses in nonprofit management also attempt to disseminate the findings of scholarly research through newsletters and published papers.

CONCLUSION

Since 1990 the number of university- and college-based graduate programs in nonprofit management in the United States has grown tremendously. In 1990 Wish found 17 such programs; in 1992 she found 32. In 1997 we determined that 76 graduate programs included three or more courses focusing on nonprofit organizations.

Although some of Wish's original 1990 conclusions are still pertinent, the current research also demonstrates a changing educational landscape. Wish's original finding about degrees and colleges still holds true: The marriage between the public and nonprofit sectors has stabilized. About 43 percent of these universities include their nonprofit organization courses in an MPA degree program housed in a college or department of public administration or in a political science department within a college of arts and sciences. Only 14 percent of the programs that offer at least three nonprofit management courses are housed in schools of business or business and public administration, although additional business schools offer one or two specialized courses. The remaining 43 percent of the graduate programs offering three or more courses in nonprofit management are located in other schools or colleges. Finally, 45 percent of the universities that offer graduate degrees emphasizing nonprofit management also offer a certificate; about two-thirds of the programs offer a certificate in nonprofit management or nonprofit management and leadership.

This census of university-based educational programs focusing on nonprofit management, which indicates the rapid growth of the field since 1990, concludes the first phase of this research project. In the second phase we examine the impact these programs have on the nonprofit sector. What skills and knowledge are taught in most of the university-based programs? What skills do practitioners perceive as most important for managing nonprofit organizations? Which of these competencies are evident in the graduates of these programs? Do the employers of these graduates perceive these competencies as important? The analysis of these questions forms the basis for the second phase of this project.

NOTES

1.   Educational programs that focus on a particular subsector of the nonprofit sector were not the target for a mailing because the research focuses on generic management for all nonprofit organizations rather than on management of organizations devoted specifically to education, arts, religion, and the like.

2.   Although some researchers would suggest that our data may significantly underrepresent the number of programs, we are confident that the data represent all graduate programs quite accurately, for the following reasons:

- The original census of programs was taken in 1990. Many academics in the field are aware of the study and since that time have sent literature about their programs to the researchers.
- Only a few networks of academics are involved with programs of this type: the Nonprofit Organization Management Education Section of NASPAA, NACC, and ARNOVA. As this study has been discussed at most annual meetings of these groups since 1992, we are confident that we have reached the programs affiliated with these networks.
- In the instructions for completing the questionnaires we stated that the results would be summarized in national publications. This avenue for publicity offered program directors an extra incentive to complete the questionnaire.

APPENDIX 2.1
UNIVERSITIES AND COLLEGES OFFERING A NONPROFIT
MANAGEMENT CONCENTRATION

COLLEGE OR UNIVERSITY	MASTER'S DEGREE OFFERED
Antioch University	Master of Human Services Administration
Auburn University at Montgomery	Master of Public Administration (MPA)
Boston University	Master of Business Administration (MBA)
Boston University School of Social Work	Master of Social Work (MSW)
Bowling Green State University	MPA
Brandeis University	Master of Management in Human Services
California State University at Hayward	MPA
Case Western Reserve University	Master of Nonprofit Organization
CUNY, Baruch College	MPA
DePaul University	Master of Science in Public Service Management (MS)
Eastern College	MBA
Florida State University	MSW
George Mason University	MPA
Georgia State University	Master in Urban Studies
Golden Gate University	Master of Arts (MA)
Grand Valley State University	MPA
Hamline University Graduate School	Master of Arts in Public Administration
Harvard University, Kennedy School	Master in Public Policy/Public Administration
Hunter College School of Social Work	MSW
Indiana University	Master of Public Affairs
Indiana University, Center on Philanthropy	MA in Philanthropic Studies
Indiana University, Purdue University	Master in Public Affairs
Kennesaw State College, Cole School of Business	MPA
Kennesaw State College, MPA Program	MS
Kent State University	MBA
Lewis and Clark College	MPA
Lindenwood College	MA in Human Services Agency Management
Long Island University	MPA
Marywood College	MPA

Moorhead State University	MS in Public and Human
	Service Administration
New School for Social Research	MS in Nonprofit Management
New York University,	
Wagner Graduate School	MPA
Northwestern University	Master of Management
Oakland University	MPA
Ohio State University	MSW
Park College	MPA
Regis University	Master of Nonprofit Management
Roberts Wesleyan College	Master of Science in
	Organizational Management
Roosevelt University	MPA
Saint Mary's University	Master of Arts in Philanthropy
of Minnesota	and Development
San Francisco State University	MPA
Seattle University	Executive Master in
	Not-For-Profit Leadership
Seton Hall University	MPA
Southern Connecticut	
State University	MSW
Southern Illinois	
University, Edwardsville	MPA
Spertus College of Judaica	Master of Science in Human Services
	Administration
St. Louis University	MSW
State University of New York at	
Albany	MPA
Temple University	Master in Social Work Administration
Tufts University	Master of Arts
University of Alabama	
at Birmingham	MPA
University of California at Berkeley	MBA
University of Colorado,	
School of Public Affairs	MS in Public Administration
University of Colorado at Denver	MPA
University of Connecticut	MPA
University of Illinois at Urbana	MSW
University of Judaism	MPA in Nonprofit Management
University of Memphis	MPA
University of Michigan	MSW in Administration
University of Minnesota, Humphrey	
Institute	Master in Public Affairs
University of Missouri at	
Kansas City	MPA
University of Missouri, St. Louis	Master in Public Policy
University of Nebraska	MPA

University of North Carolina at Chapel Hill	MPA
University of Northern Iowa	Master of Arts
University of Notre Dame	Master of Science in Administration
University of Pittsburgh	MPA
University of San Francisco	Master of Nonprofit Administration
University of Southern California	MPA
University of St. Thomas	MBA
University of Washington, MPA Program	MPA
University of Washington School of Social Work	MSW
University of West Florida	MPA
Western Michigan University	MPA
Widener University	MPA
Yeshiva University	MSW

3

Dilemmas Facing Nonprofit Management Education: The Australian Example

Mark Lyons

NONPROFIT ORGANIZATIONS IN AUSTRALIA

Australia, with a population of 18 million, has a large nonprofit sector. Overall, nonprofit organizations in Australia employ about 10 percent of private sector employees (Lyons, 1994). There are at least 400,000 nonprofit organizations, but few of these, only about 50,000 in all, are employers. Nonprofit organizations are the dominant form of organization in four industries: social services, sport and recreation, interest groups (trade and professional associations and advocacy organizations), and, of course, religious institutions. Nonprofits are significant providers of services in the health industry, education, hospitality, and the arts. They also have an important presence in the finance and insurance industry, though in these industries they inevitably take a mutual benefit form. Some scholars would exclude mutuals from the nonprofit universe; but such a definition would not reduce estimates of the size of Australia's nonprofit sector by much, as mutuals contribute less than 10 percent of nonprofit employment.

Nonprofit organizations display certain characteristics that set them apart from for-profit organizations and government organizations. These characteristics pose special challenges for their managers. Although not all nonprofit organizations display all these characteristics to the same degree, it is generally accepted, nonetheless, that nonprofit organizations

- are value-driven in some particular way;
- utilize and depend upon voluntary labor;
- obtain their revenue from a wide range of sources and that much of that revenue is not generated from the sale of goods and services but is obtained from third parties;
- give an especially important role to boards of governors, either as representatives of the membership or as representatives of, and thus having a special duty to, the wider community; this in turn makes the relationship between board and chief executive a particularly problematic one;

- generally lack simple criteria for assessing their performance. Certainly, profit or return on funds invested, so relatively easy to use in the for-profit sector, cannot apply. (O'Neill and Young, 1988; Mason, 1984)

These characteristics generate and shape practical problems of organizational management, both of human and of financial resources. Yet it should be noted that some of these distinctive characteristics, such as the difficulty of judging perform-ance, are shared with government bodies and may be a characteristic of the type of service provided rather than the organizational form. Indeed, it should be noted that each of the industries where nonprofits are particularly active has a number of in-dustry-specific features as well, features that shape the particular challenges to man-agers in each industry, irrespective of the type or sector of the organization being managed.

The tension between an industry and a sector focus is the main theme of this chapter. It is a theme that was extensively explored in a United States context by Paul DiMaggio at the first nonprofit management education conference in 1986. He noted a tension between generalist and specialist (or industry-specific) nonprofit management training and claimed that it was impossible to resolve arguments about the appropriateness of one or the other focus other than conjecturally (DiMaggio, 1988). Since then, little has been done to explore empirically the dilemmas he noted.

MANAGEMENT EDUCATION AND TRAINING IN AUSTRALIA

Management education and training in Australia is provided in many forms by many different organizations. Universities offer bachelor's degrees (three years of full-time study) or postgraduate courses, ranging from six months to two years of full-time study in business, administration, or management. Technical and further education (TAFE) colleges teach one- or two-year certificate or diploma courses in personnel or business management, generally to part-time students. In addition, there are many short courses, ranging in length from one day to several weeks, of-fered by training consultants and by large firms to their employees.

This short summary immediately raises a number of knotty issues frequently de-bated in Australia: Is there a difference between education and training? Can man-agers be trained or only educated? Can young undergraduates with little or no expe-rience of organizational life or of management be educated (or trained) for manage-ment?

In practice, a distinction between education and training is recognized. It is usu-ally described as having to do with the depth and extent of knowledge transmitted, the extent to which analytical and appreciative skills are taught, and the level of ca-pacity for self-aware, self-initiated action that is expected of a person completing a particular course of study. But the boundaries are blurred. Many would say that management cannot be taught to young people, but plenty of university business and commerce courses try to teach it anyhow. Short courses are generally tailored for people occupying positions with at least some supervisory component. At this level, they usually focus on particular management skills such as "conflict resolution" or "team building" or "negotiation skills." However, short courses also include one-week intensive residential programs for chief executives of middle-size or large companies. Management courses in technical or community colleges, like the majority of short courses, tend to focus on identifiable management competencies (Australian postsecondary education and training outside of universities is currently in the grip of the competency standards movement). Despite their claim to identify and standardize generic management competencies, these appear at times to reflect the particular needs of for-profit organizations, especially small business. For example, a good deal of emphasis is placed on marketing and pricing, presuming that the survival of the business depended upon successfully selling in a highly competitive marketplace.

Within universities, the picture is somewhat different. Undergraduate courses in management generally build their education on a foundation of business or management disciplines: accounting, finance, economics, law, marketing, communication, and human resource management. To this foundation they add a more extended study of organizational and management subjects, such as organizational culture, organizational change, history of management thought, corporate strategy, strategic management, and business policy.

At the graduate level, by far the most popular management course is the MBA. All 38 universities in Australia teach an MBA program. MBA programs provide students with an introduction to a range of business or management functions, including economics, finance, accounting, human resources, marketing, and law. Invariably they include some quantitative skills, as so many of the functional areas depend on quantitative analysis. They provide an opportunity for students to study one or two of these areas at greater depth and generally make some attempt, via capstone subjects or case studies, to encourage students to integrate these skills. They invariably assume that students will be taking management positions in large for-profit organizations. Both full-time and part-time programs are offered. Most students have had at least 10 years of business experience, some much more. However, the average age and experience of MBA students is trending downward. A recent review of management education and training in Australia found that none of these courses could be described as world-class and that while they were strong in providing technical functional skills such as finance, they were not so strong on strategic and entrepreneurial skills and were weak in the area of people management (Industry Task Force on Leadership and Management Skills, 1995).

In addition to generalist management programs for for-profit managers, there are a few graduate courses preparing people for management positions in nonprofit organizations and a somewhat larger number for management positions in the public sector.

As well as these generalist courses, there are other graduate courses that prepare students for management positions in particular organizational functions, such as finance management, human resource management, and marketing management. These invariably assume that the students will be employed in for-profit firms. Altogether, it has been estimated that over 17,000 students are enrolled in postgraduate management courses provided by university management or business schools (Industry Task Force on Leadership and Management Skills, 1995).

Finally, there are many graduate courses that seek to prepare students for management positions in particular industries. These usually assume and build on a previous professional preparation obtained at an undergraduate level or previous post-graduate training. Such courses include education administration, nursing admini-stration, health services management, arts management, sports management, manu-facturing management, tourism management, agribusiness management, social ad-ministration, and human services management. Interestingly, with a few exceptions, these are from industries in which nonprofit organizations (both government and private) are major providers and in which professionals or elite performers define the parameters and practices of the industry.

NONPROFIT MANAGEMENT EDUCATION

The first specialist nonprofit management education course in Australia was an associate diploma in community organizations, commenced by what is now the Uni-versity of Technology, Sydney (UTS), in 1986. It was designed to respond to a need for some formal education in management expressed by many people occupying management positions in small and medium-sized nonprofit social service organiza-tions. Most people holding such positions had no previous postsecondary education, and many had come into their current management positions after considerable vol-untary experience as managers.

However, as it became clear that there were many others in management positions in nonprofit social service organizations who had already obtained undergraduate qualifications, in 1991 a master's program was begun. It was taught only on a part-time basis, and to gain entry students had to be working in nonprofit organiza-tions. It was designed along the generalist lines of an MBA program, providing an introduction to a range of management functions such as financial management, marketing, and human resource management, as well as to subjects such as fund-raising management that were peculiar to nonprofit organizations. Even the func-tionally specific subjects were taught in a way that addressed directly the particular issues and problems faced by managers of nonprofit organizations. Although sev-eral of these were also available to students in a public management program, that latter program was taught at another campus and few chose to attend classes on the subjects taught to the nonprofit management students. Since 1991 the UTS master's program has taken in about 30 new students per year. Almost all of these have come from nonprofits in the social services industry. It is taught only on a part-time basis, requiring students to attend university for an afternoon and evening, or two evenings per week. Students must have had at least two years' experience working in non-profit organizations since graduation, but most have had at least 10 years and some as many as 30.

Since that time, four other Australian universities have begun master's programs or parts of master's programs designed for managers of nonprofit organizations. The second began at the University of New England (UNE) in 1993. It is a specializa-tion of three subjects within a 14-subject generalist MBA degree. It is taught by distance mode on a part-time basis. Initially designed for managers of trade and professional associations, it soon adapted its curriculum to cater to students in social service organizations, since these constituted approximately half its initial intake. Another program began at the Royal Melbourne Institute of Technology (RMIT) in 1995. It is focused on managers of social services and includes public sector workers as well. It is a specialization within a larger degree program for people working in public and nonprofit organizations. It seeks to provide a critical understanding of management and does not teach any of the generic management skills such as marketing, accounting, human resource management, and the like. The other two programs, services administration and a nonprofit management specialization in a Master of Public Management degree, have only just begun, at the University of Notre Dame Australia in Fremantle, Western Australia, and at Monash University in Melbourne. It would appear that the Notre Dame program is aimed at students from a wide range of service industries, which would include for-profit and public sector providers as well as those in nonprofit organizations. The Monash course is a four-subject specialization in a 14-subject public management program. The Australian Society of Association Executives sponsors a one-week residential short course in associations management, run each year by a management training institute associated with Monash University.

Of these five master's courses, only the UTS course is designed exclusively for nonprofit managers; indeed, it excludes people working in government departments from the core components of the course. The other courses are specializations of existing programs directed at students working in government or for-profit settings. Only the UNE specialization and, probably, the University of Notre Dame program are clearly directed at students working in nonprofit organizations in a wide range of industries. However, the UNE course attracts students from two industries: interest groups and social services. The UTS program has been marketed only to prospective students in nonprofit social service organizations and, for the most part, only attracts students from those settings. All told, these five courses, or specializations, enrolled fewer than 200 students in 1996-97.

The overall picture of nonprofit management education in Australia is that

- it is a relatively new field of endeavor;
- with one exception, it is presented as a specialization in courses that are designed for students in for-profit and/or government organizations;
- it attracts students in nonprofits in only two industries (interest groups and social services; the Notre Dame Australia program may expand beyond this);
- none of the courses tries to provide an education for managers of nonprofit organizations in all industries and across all management skills in the way that many MBA courses do, or claim to do, for for-profit managers;
- there is some ambiguity about what nonprofit management education should include: for two courses (RMIT and Notre Dame), it is not clear that the design of any subject is based on an assumption that there are some special features of nonprofit organizations that need to be addressed and which generate a need for specifically nonprofit management education.

The continuing financial pressure experienced by Australian universities, as levels of government subsidies fail to keep pace with increasing student numbers, means that all courses with small enrollments ("boutique courses," as they are sometimes called) are constantly under threat of closure. What appears to be the beginning of a growth of nonprofit management education in Australia may be short-lived.

OTHER MANAGEMENT EDUCATION FOR NONPROFIT MANAGERS

Although data are not available, it seems not unreasonable to assume that many more than 200 managers, or likely managers, of nonprofit organizations will be enrolled in management courses that pay no specific attention to any special characteristics of nonprofit organizations as a class or organizational sector.

A few will be enrolled in generalist MBA or functional specialties such as marketing or human resource management. However, most will be enrolled in industry-specific management courses. In 1994, 20 Australian universities provided graduate courses in education administration or management; 11 offered courses in health services administration or management; four offered sports management; and three offered arts management. All told, in 1994, these courses enrolled over 3,000 students (Department of Employment, Education and Training, 1995). A smaller number of students studied in similar courses, or specialties in more general courses, at the undergraduate level.

Students in all of these courses are seeking a course that will provide them an education in management. A majority or a large minority of organizations in each of these industries consists of nonprofit organizations. Yet examination of a sample of course material indicates a total lack of any kind of sectoral sensitivity. There would appear to be no awareness in any of these courses of any specific management issues that might emerge from the nonprofit character of many of the organizations being managed.

This point can be illustrated by two examples. In the field of sports management, a great deal of attention is devoted to what is characterized as professional versus volunteer conflict. What is being referred to is conflict between paid (and hopefully professionally educated) managers and volunteer boards. It is an important issue, as during the 1980s many national and state-level sporting associations obtained sufficient financing to enable them to appoint professional management staff. Prior to that, they relied for their management on volunteer boards. The direct relevance to these matters of a long-established literature on board/CEO relations from the field of nonprofit scholarship would seem obvious, but this literature does not appear in any of the course reading lists and is rarely cited in research (Auld, 1995).

Another example is the arts industry, in which fundraising is a major source of revenue for both nonprofit and government organizations. Yet none of the courses in arts management appears to include a course on fundraising or development management as part of the curriculum.

Many of these industry-specific courses include specialized law subjects in their curriculum, but these appear to relate entirely to legislative issues arising from features of the industry rather than from the nonprofit character of many of the organizations in that industry. They all include a financial management course, but this is either geared for public sector students, as in education administration or health services management courses, or borrowed from MBA programs, where the emphasis is on corporate financial management.

WHY IS AUSTRALIAN NONPROFIT MANAGEMENT EDUCATION SO WEAK?

The overall impression is clear. In Australia, despite nonprofit organizations being important, even dominant, parts of several major industries, the need for specialized nonprofit management education is barely recognized. There are several reasons for this.

Perhaps the most significant reason is the dominance of an industry focus among both students and educators. In those industries where nonprofits are numerous, most staff occupying management positions begin as professionals or highly skilled practitioners (teachers, nurses, social workers, doctors, athletes, artists, and performers). There is some evidence that managers who have not been practitioners are likely to be rejected by the professional workforce (Auld, 1995). As people enter employment in the industry as professionals, the major management task is seen as managing other professionals. Many of the university faculties and schools that provide an initial professional education at an undergraduate level also provide graduate management education within that field. Professional practice need not be sector aware. Teaching is teaching whether it is in a government or a private school; so, too, nursing and medicine are largely indifferent to whether the hospital or health center is government, for-profit, or nonprofit. Therefore, because a manager is seen primarily as a person responsible for managing professional service providers, the task of management and the context of management education remain focused on that practice rather than on the organization that employs both service provider and manager.

Although management tasks may vary considerably depending on the auspice of the organization being managed, management education that grows out of professional education is largely indifferent to this specificity; and many professionals who move into management positions are initially indifferent to it as well. Even when their experience provides some awareness of difference, they do not see a particular need to specialize in the management of nonprofit organizations (or government organizations, for that matter) since they see their career path as remaining within that industry and thus, possibly, taking them from nonprofit to government to perhaps for-profit organizations. Their desire for management education is to equip them to manage within that industry rather than across industries within the same sector. One consequence of this focus on managing within a context of professional practice is that such courses are often less than adequate in their treatment of basic management disciplines such as financial management or organizational theory.

An industry-specific focus need not preclude management education within a particular industry from reflecting the sectoral composition of the industry. In practice, however, management education in specific professions or industries assumes, usually incorrectly, that the organizations being managed are either government or for-profit. It is at this point that the absence of three preconditions for strong nonprofit management education become evident. These preconditions are an institutional structure for the Australian nonprofit sector, a generally accepted terminology to describe nonprofits, and a widely focused nonprofit literature that speaks to nonprofit managers in many industries.

Australia possesses a large number of what are called "peak councils" claiming to speak for and sometimes to coordinate the activity of its many nonprofit organizations, but these are all industry or subindustry specific: social services, health services, school education, conservation, trade and professional associations, and so on. There is no body that brings them all together and thus no body to provide a focus for the nonprofit sector as a whole. It might be noted that the business sector does not possess a single peak either. There are many thousands of trade and industry associations, but above these are far fewer peaks. It only takes four peak bodies to speak for the great majority of Australia's 600,000 business organizations: large corporations, medium-sized enterprises, small business, and farm organizations. It might also be noted that no country appears to possess a single body to speak for the nonprofit sector. Independent Sector in the United States perhaps comes closest, but it nonetheless is shaped by the institutional divisions created by U.S. tax law and excludes trade and industry associations and many community interest groups from its purview. Nonetheless, the high level of segmentation of Australia's nonprofit sector works against the emergence of a nonprofit sector identity and against a concept of nonprofit management education.

Terminological profligacy also works against the emergence of a concept of "nonprofit sector." In Australia no single term to describe nonprofit organizations is widely accepted. Terminology to describe that class of organization tends to be industry specific. Sometimes several terms are used interchangeably within the one industry: "community," "charitable," "nongovernmental" or "nonprofit" within the social services; "private" in education; "private" (which also covers for-profit hospitals) in health and, increasingly, "foundation"; "club" or "society" in the sports and recreation and hospitality industries; "association" or "nonprofit" in interest groups; and "foundation" in research.

There is little Australian literature on nonprofit organizations and their management. For the most part, that which exists is restricted to social service nonprofits. As well, the burgeoning international literature on nonprofit organizations has some major gaps. Much of that literature also is specific to a few related industries such as the social services, health, the arts, churches, and trade associations. Very little work has been done on sport and recreation, trade unions and political parties, or mutual finance organizations. Even less cross-industry work has been done. This may be because most research has been done in the United States, where, for example, sporting organizations are mostly for-profit firms and where political parties seem generally to be considered not truly nonprofit. These conditions do not apply in continental Europe, but language differences constrain the influence any literature from that source might have.

Attempts to develop a theory of nonprofit organizations by and large restrict themselves to public-serving nonprofits. They generally exclude self-help and membership associations, despite their political and social importance, and generally define mutuals as outside the nonprofit sector.

Much of the development of nonprofit theory over the past two decades has been driven by economists. At its best, it attempts to encompass nonprofit organizations from the various industries where they are active, but in doing so it either remains at an abstract level that speaks clearly only to economists (for example, Steinberg, 1993) or provides illustrations or evidence drawn from only one or two industries (Weisbrod, 1988). Others, such as Gassler (1990), focus attention only on public benefit nonprofits. Theories developed by sociologists and political scientists tend to take different organizations as a starting point. Some, such as the theory of Billis (1993) about the implications of organizational growth, are relevant to most nonprofits; but others, such as Wood's (1992) life cycle theory, while evocative, appear to apply to nonprofits with only a certain type of governance. Lohmann (1989, p. 372) develops his theory of the commons via a focus on "donative-mutual associations, societies, congregations, groups, and other similar forms of collectives." This line of theory speaks to many in the nonprofit sector who feel alienated from economic theory; but it does not speak to the managers of many nonprofits, such as hospitals, childcare centers, or social clubs, that provide services in highly competitive markets. There is a body of scholarship in the United States that draws from political science and sociology and does focus on mutual associations (for example, O'Neill, 1994; Smith, 1993), but this tradition has generally been eclipsed over the past twenty years, although the rapidly growing interest in social capital and civil society may change this (Lyons, 1996).

It should also be noted that within the mainstream literature on nonprofit organizations there is doubt expressed from time to time about whether there really is a nonprofit sector or whether nonprofit organizations are a distinct class of organizations. These claims usually resolve around two points:

- whether it makes any sense to group into a single sector organizations as diverse as, for example, a large hospital, a play group, a women's shelter, a mosque, and a trade association;
- that many so-called nonprofit organizations are in reality hybrids, employing characteristics drawn from for-profit or government organizations and, perhaps, being significantly suffused with government authority; the preferred approach is to study these organizational forms without assuming any ideal type or archetype of nonprofit (or for-profit or government) organization.

Both these points have merit but do not fatally weaken the nonprofit case. A good deal of difference can be observed between what are generally called nonprofit organizations without damaging the claim that these organizations have some features in common that affect their organizational behavior and differentiate them from for-profit and government organizations and without forcing abandonment of that type of organization. Indeed, if reference to nonprofit organization were to be abandoned, then, for the same reasons, so too could be reference to for-profit and governmental organizations. Yet, to do this would be to weaken significantly our capacity to explore and analyze organizational life.

While the strange hybrid types of organizations that are emerging in some industries are certainly interesting, presumably what makes them interesting and allows them to be identified as hybrids is that they are, or appear to be, mixtures of two (or more) of the ideal or archetypal organizations.

WHAT CAN BE DONE?

Nonprofit management education in Australia is at an embryonic stage. Whether or not it grows will depend on actions taken over the next few years by those who are its champions. If they believe there is a common core of knowledge and a suite of skills needed by anyone who would manage a nonprofit organization in whatever industry the organization is active, then they need to build a course around this belief.

Of equal importance, they should recognize that many managers of nonprofit organizations will continue to receive their management education in industry-specific courses. Those who espouse a common nonprofit management education should endeavor to use research and writing to convince those offering specialist courses that there are merits in recognizing the distinctive characteristics of nonprofit organizations and the distinctive problems these generate for managers irrespective of the industry they are managing in. Perhaps the best way to do this is via joint seminars and comparative (cross-industry) research projects.

In the longer term, it will be important that those who are seeking to develop a more comprehensive theory of nonprofit organizations take account of the variety of industries nonprofit organizations are active in. This will mean bridging not only the gap between the public-serving and the member-serving organizations but also the disciplinary gap between economics on the one hand and sociology and political science on the other, since each discipline tends to focus on particular sets of nonprofits as the site for theory development. As with the proposal for cross-industry dialogue, cross-disciplinary dialogue is important, too. The quest for a single, all-encompassing theory of nonprofit organization is almost certainly an impossible one, but its pursuit will generate much enlightenment for scholars and practitioners if it is conducted with openness and genuine curiosity.

In Australia, at least, we have a long way to go. I expect that the rest of the world does, too.

4

Opening Up Nonprofit Management Development: Lessons from the Open University's Voluntary Sector Management Programme

Chris Cornforth, Rob Paton, and Julian Batsleer

INTRODUCTION

The Open University's Voluntary Sector Management Programme (VSMP) has arguably been the largest and most significant initiative in accredited nonprofit management education in the last decade. This distance learning program is unique in several respects:

- the *amount of time and resources* committed: over £1,000,000 of public and charitable funds were invested over a five-year period;
- the extent of *collaboration with practitioners* in both course development and delivery;
- the *scale of operation:* between 1991 and 1997 nearly 3,000 nonprofit managers studied courses in the program; in 1997 some 600 managers registered for these courses;
- the extent of *international diffusion* of the program: the courses have been taken by managers in at least 10 other countries in Central and Western Europe and Africa;
- the *accessibility* of the program to managers from disadvantaged groups, living in rural areas, or with disabilities;
- the extent and variety of *formal evaluations* of the program, including a wide range of independently gathered data on its reception and long-term impact.

The Open University was established in England in 1969 as a national university based exclusively on supported distance learning. It remains the world's leading distance teaching institution. The university's teaching uses a variety of different media and methods, including specially prepared booklets, video and audio tapes, software packages, television and radio programs, and face-to-face methods such as local tutorials and short-term residential schools. Computer conferencing is increasingly being used to support students in their studies and as a delivery vehicle. Open University courses are offered throughout continental western Europe. The university has partnership arrangements with organizations in most of Eastern and

Central Europe, the Far East, and several African countries. Courses in the VSMP are offered twice a year to students throughout the United Kingdom (U.K.) and in several other countries.

The case of the VSMP is interesting not just because of its size but also because it throws light on a number of key issues facing nonprofit management educators (O'Neill and Young, 1988). The main focus of this chapter is a discussion of these issues, which include:

- the sources and distinctive content of nonprofit management education;
- whether nonprofit management programs should be free-standing or part of more general management programs;
- the academic level of nonprofit management education and its contribution to professional development;
- the applicability and viability of distance-taught courses in this field and some of the particular problems and constraints they face;
- the advantages and disadvantages of locating such a program within a business school.

This chapter reviews the origins and development of the VSMP, focusing on the philosophy and pedagogical approach that influenced the overall program design, and examines the issues just outlined and what lessons can be drawn from the case. While generalizations from one case are necessarily limited, we will argue that the VSMP offers compelling evidence about the potential for distance learning courses in this area. The chapter also challenges some conventional wisdom about the location and desired level of nonprofit management education programs.

THE DEVELOPMENT OF THE PROGRAM

The VSMP was established in 1989 as a teaching and research unit within the Open University's Business School (OUBS). The VSMP's mission has been to develop and deliver a nationally accessible and accredited management curriculum for those exercising administrative responsibilities across the spectrum of voluntary and nonprofit enterprises in the U.K. This section describes key aspects of the development of the program.

Establishing the VSMP

Management has long been a key issue in discussions of the changing roles and identities of voluntary organizations (Handy, 1981). Even in the late 1980s, however, the relevant literature was still predominantly in the form of prescriptive "how to do it" manuals. There was little serious research and critical reflection, no language adequate for the concerns of both researchers and practitioners, and no coordinated national framework for management development. "Voluntary sector management" was largely ignored by MBA programs and remained a ghetto within programs in social and public administration. The mid 1980s had seen a growth of short courses for practitioners provided by individual trainers and consultants. However, beyond the networking activities of centers such as the National Council for Voluntary Organisations and the in-house programs of a very few large national agencies, there was a marked absence of programs of sustained development for the growing cohorts of professional managers and paid staff within a diffuse but in-creasingly important sector.

Initial funding for a teaching program came from a private charitable trust. The trust was led by a far-sighted businessman and philanthropist whose close involve-ment with the sector over many years had led him to recognize the need for more management education; he had developed the idea of "a management school for the voluntary sector." He contacted the Open University, where work on voluntary sec-tor management had already begun (Paton and Hooker, 1990), and quickly recog-nized the advantage of investing in a distance learning institution whose courses were available nationally, with the potential to reach hundreds rather than tens of students. His support and willingness to take a big risk meant that in 1988 staff could begin a major exercise in market research, consultation, curriculum design, and fundraising.

At this time the British government was promoting markets and managerialism in social policy. This was reflected in initiatives related to the voluntary sector (Home Office, 1989, 1990). Hence in early 1989 VSMP staff were able to present detailed plans to the Voluntary Service Unit at the Home Office, knowing that an initiative to support management development in the sector was being planned. The Home Of-fice brokered a consortium of seven government departments to fund three initia-tives, of which the VSMP was the largest. Later, the VSMP also attracted donations from major British companies.

The distinctive contours of the program as it developed were shaped by the inter-play of three key factors.

Market demands and aspirations. Market research identified widespread demand for courses that addressed directly the experiences, needs, and aspirations of junior and middle managers in large organizations and the paid professional staff with management responsibilities from small and medium-sized organizations (who, at that time, did not necessarily define themselves as "managers"). This required sus-tained and accessible development opportunities beyond the level of short courses but not as restricted or exclusive as a very few master's programs available mainly to a small number of senior executives. A program for the fast-growing cohorts of junior and middle managers would also be likely to have the greatest impact on im-proving management performance generally across the sector. Although VSMP's core organizational market was defined as the "traditional" U.K. welfare-focused voluntary sector, the research also identified some important secondary markets in other types of nonprofit, value-based organizations: housing associations, trade unions, churches, small arts organizations, and environmental campaigns.

Management qualifications. Early consultations had prompted a well-articulated demand for access to "proper management" learning and qualifications; VSMP was asked to present a management curriculum that was generic but addressed the spe-cific circumstances and concerns of nonprofit management. This meant that VSMP was deliberately located within the OU's new Business School. Its courses were designed to sit within the open-access, modular professional programs that OUBS had been evolving since the mid 1980s, as part of the emerging national framework of transferable management qualifications. These programs provide a ladder of op-portunity for those without prior educational credit; the open-entry certificate is the first half of the diploma, and the diploma is one means of entry to the MBA.

Financial and operational feasibility. The OU's reputation as the world's premier distance teaching university rests on the quality of the distinctive forms of supported learning it provides. Achieving that quality is, however, comparatively costly within the distance education arena. The VSMP had to secure significant levels of external financial support for the initial investment in course development. Moreover, its real success would hinge on the subsequent capacity of the program to be self-financing. This entailed attracting at least 500 students a year for sustained six-month, 220-hour courses involving financial and time commitments well above those that low-income voluntary organizations and their managers had been accustomed to making for management development.

Designing and Delivering VSMP's Curriculum and Courses

The curriculum design and consultation process led to the definition of two new, sector-specific, certificate-level courses: Managing Voluntary and Non-Profit Enterprises (MVNE) and Winning Resources and Support (WRS). To overcome "ghettoization," these were supplemented by the addition of sector-related materials in a third certificate course, Accounting for Managers, together with a longer-term process of ensuring that *all* OUBS courses at subsequent diploma and MBA levels take account of the management learning needs and context of "third sector" students and organizations. This longer-term project continues and has not been without its difficulties. Nevertheless, considerable progress has been made; indeed, each year a small number of OUBS students from private companies complain that too much attention is given to nonprofit issues in the generic courses.

The content of these two sector-specific courses has been the keystone of VSMP's teaching intervention. The construction and delivery of both these courses were not just a matter of "versioning" or "contextualization"; they were based on original research and, in different ways, both entailed a major recasting of conventional management syllabi. They also went well beyond the existing professional "how to do it" literature for nonprofit management. For example, WRS elaborates a conceptual framework for the analysis and practice of many key topics and concerns in fundraising, campaigning, and marketing by bringing together clusters of techniques that are usually perceived and taught as quite separate areas of competence and understanding (Paton, 1996).

The OU's standard procedures for course production and presentation lent themselves to a collaborative process of curriculum development between different stakeholders: a core group of OUBS academic staff, voluntary organization representatives, potential students and tutors, and external academic and professional assessors and validators. This resulted in a group of courses informed by a distinctive "voice" or "stance," which enhanced their relevance and acceptability for students working in a sector noted for its flux, diversity, and doubts about the values associated with "management." That "voice" derived from a consonance between two factors: VSMP's underlying philosophy of management and management learning and the use of OUBS pedagogical methods of supported distance learning in professional development.

Philosophy

VSMP's central philosophy grew out of approaches to management and to individual and organizational learning that are articulated in the work of such figures as Argyris and Schon (1978), Schon (1984), Mintzberg (1987), and Senge (1990). Management is not an exact science. Managers are confronted with an inherent tension between a rational/instrumental view of management and the nature of management as a negotiated social process. The reality of the manager's experience, particularly within nonprofit organizations, is that she or he is faced with incomplete information, differences of perception and meaning, and conflicting agendas and interests. Contrary to the often dominant impression (and self-perception) of many voluntary agencies as essentially unitary organizations held together and driven forward by shared commitments to core values and principles, managers actually have to operate in a world of uncertainties, dilemmas, and ambiguities. Once one probes behind the surface rhetoric, the distinctive value bases of voluntary organizations are often a source of real and irreconcilable differences (Paton, 1995). Hence VSMP's courses consistently acknowledged the messy, uncertain, political, and value-based nature of management.

It is not, therefore, the aim of VSMP courses to inculcate "good practice" or pass on an essentially prescriptive set of behaviors and analyses. The courses explicitly challenge some of the conventional management theories and practices. Equally important, however, the program invites students to critique the often deeply held beliefs and expectations of those working in voluntary organizations that there is a "right" way for voluntary organizations to organize their affairs.

Although students become familiar with many practical recipes and techniques and study mainstream management ideas and theories, a central focus is on understanding situations. The courses aim to present a repertoire of frameworks and theories that enable students to make sense of their experience and sharpen their judgments about what is appropriate and feasible in the *specific* circumstances and organizations in which they find themselves.

The VSMP's philosophy of management is complemented by a pedagogy and course design that enable a distance-taught program to speak effectively to students from very different types of organizations who bring radically divergent perceptions, prior experiences, and languages to their management learning.

The Open University's approach to supported distance learning provides a framework within which to present a set of learning dialogues. Through a mixture of structured activities, self-assessment questions, and (crucially) experience-based assignments, students are required to engage intellectually with new ideas, concepts, theories, and debates and to explore how those concepts could illuminate their practice. This dialogue means that each course is not an abstract, academic exercise but a sustained six-month program of professional development.

The central dialogue is primarily driven by the individually managed interplay between the theories introduced through the various course components and technologies and the student's own context and experience. A second key dialogue takes place between student and tutor. Each student has access—by phone, correspondence, and, in some instances, e-mail—to an individual tutor who is contracted not just to grade and comment on assignments but to act as a personal mentor to each of his or her students. In many respects, the individual student-tutor dialogue in a

VSMP course is more intense and more significant than that which evolves within the more "normal" setting of the face-to-face seminars and workshops, in which individual relationships are mediated through dominant group processes.

Through a regular program of group tutorials and a compulsory residential school, a third key dialogue is that among students themselves: the sharing of experience and the establishment of safe environments within which to practice skills and explore some of the problems and dilemmas posed both by their experience of management and the sometimes painful and challenging learning taking place as a result of the course.

A fourth dialogue is that among the students, colleagues, and other professionals in the organizations with which they worked and more broadly in the sector. This has been most successful and explicit in those larger organizations that have adopted the program as a major vehicle for staff and management development, creating in-house study groups and supporting them with additional seminars, meetings with directors, project activities, and the like.

Together these elements of philosophy and pedagogy came to be expressed in a "voice" or stance that

- was positive without being glib or facile;
- was realistic about difficulties and limitations without being cynical;
- offered useful tools without being prescriptive or universalist;
- validated experience and perceptions but also challenged students to reconsider;
- affirmed the value of understanding difficulties even when they have no very obvious resolution.

Outcomes

The VSMP was planned, funded, and justified as a national initiative designed to have a substantial and lasting impact. Achieving this meant, at a minimum,

- attracting sufficient students to register for (*and complete*) the courses, to make it a permanent and self-financing feature of the OUBS programs;
- ensuring that the experience of study was found relevant and rewarding.

Contrary to the expectations of many at the time the program was announced, over 500 students a year register in the program. This enrollment level is not yet quite as high as the program staff originally forecast. The marketing challenge was underestimated, as is discussed hereafter. Course completion rates have never fallen below 80 percent of finally registered students and are usually well above that level.

The courses have been repeatedly and independently evaluated from their inception, both by external bodies—for example, funders and employers sponsoring students—and by staff of the University's Institute of Educational Technology. Studies over the first two years of MVNE were reviewed and summarized by Burt (1994), who also drew on unsolicited student correspondence and his own visits and telephone interviews. He reported

- unusually high levels of perceived interest, relevance, and satisfaction during the course, notwithstanding the heavy demands it made on students' time;

- many reports of perceived practical benefits in the workplace;
- high levels of appreciation at the end of the course.

Responses to one question in particular indicate the breadth and depth of appreciation among students. Since many managers sample a range of management courses and programs in the course of their careers, one way of gauging the value of courses is to ask them to make comparative assessments. Students in two surveys were asked to compare the VSMP course against the best of the other management courses they had taken, in terms of value for time and money. The results were as follows: 54 percent of respondents rated the course as much better value, 30 percent as somewhat better value, 13 percent as about the same, and 3 percent as somewhat less value.

This report has since been confirmed by comparable evaluations of WRS. Most significantly, it is confirmed by repeat business from many organizations and the overwhelming importance of word-of-mouth recommendation in the decision to enroll.

But the popularity of a program does not necessarily mean that it enhances management practice. An evaluation has to consider whether there is evidence that the program actually leads to benefits for the colleagues, organizations, and clients of those who study it. In addition to anecdotal evidence (for example, the student who said he took the course "because of the difference I saw it made in my boss") a follow-up study of MVNE, which was designed to assess course impact 16 months after course completion, found that although managers reported some fading of the course ideas, the vast majority claimed a substantial continuing impact (Burt, 1994). More significant,

- they were readily able to recall and describe specific instances in the previous month when their approach had been shaped by course ideas, often in relation to significant issues;
- they had referred back to the course materials (indeed, 28 percent of respondents reported doing so at least monthly);
- they had often shared the course with colleagues (for example, by lending materials).

DISCUSSION

The VSMP can been seen as a case that throws light on a number of important questions that face educators developing programs for nonprofit managers. This section focuses on some of these questions and draws out the lessons from the VSMP experience.

Sources and Content of Nonprofit Management

In very broad terms, the search for appropriate management discourses and practices was approached from three main directions (Batsleer, 1995). One strand, which developed out of teaching and research in areas of social policy and public administration, tended to locate key management issues at the level of sectoral strategy and policy. It sought to steer voluntary organizations along their own unique, value-driven road, keeping clear of the dangerous highways of state bureaucracy and market opportunism (Billis, 1993).

A second strand, fueled in some measure by a political suspicion of "management," emerged from traditions of alternative forms of organization, community organization, and self-activity. Those involved in co-operatives, trade unions, campaigning organizations, community development organizations, and women's and black organizations sought to develop and share new, more democratic modes of organization and working practices.

A third discernible strand began to examine more critically the assumed distinctions between sectors. It drew freely, but not uncritically, on mainstream management writing, focusing attention on the complexity and diversity of voluntary organizations and the tensions they faced. This approach sought to forge a language for voluntary sector management that did not simply echo debates about social policy or uncritically reinforce voluntary organizations' self-perception of their unique values and practices (Batsleer, Cornforth, and Paton, 1991).

If the resulting course content is compared with a (notional) standard management syllabus, it is clear, first, that some standard concepts and approaches are presented unchanged but with very different illustrations and cases. Second, some concepts have been extended or developed to match circumstances that commonly arise in voluntary organizations; for example, regarding job design, it was suggested that overrich and unbounded jobs may be at least as much of an issue as narrow and impoverished jobs. Third, some concepts were introduced that would normally be included in more advanced courses (for example, concerning organizational governance and strategy). Fourth, some original concepts were introduced—for example, concerning the nature of value issues and their implications for nonprofit managers (Paton, 1995).

The implications are clear: The pressures in nonprofit management education are toward a fuller, more demanding curriculum. This was certainly the case with the VSMP, which clearly expects more of its students than its "sister" courses in the Certificate Programme.

Distinctive Concentration or Separate Program?

There were educational, market, and pragmatic reasons for developing the VSMP as a concentration rather than a freestanding program. A freestanding program probably would not be economically viable, given the large student numbers that Open University distance learning courses need to attract. Also, students appreciate the greater choices and scope for continuation that the current arrangements provide, as well as the opportunity to mix with and learn from managers in other sectors. Finally, the concentration puts the program in a position of contributing to other programs in the school rather than competing with them, thus helping secure its long-term future.

However, this endorsement of the concentration strategy must be qualified. The work of influencing other courses within the school's programs to take more account of the needs of nonprofit managers has had mixed results and is proving to be a long-term undertaking. The two main courses in which this has been tried are a marketing and an accounting course in the Certificate Programme. In both cases, part-time consultants were employed to work on the course teams over a prolonged period, since faculty working on the VSMP were already fully committed. In the case of the marketing course, this strategy worked quite well. It has proven more problematic in the accounting course. The course now includes many nonprofit examples and is more "user friendly" to nonprofit students. However, some of the main conceptual differences between management accounting in business and non-profit contexts—for example, the importance of fund accounting—have not been adequately addressed. Somewhat similar difficulties were experienced when efforts were made to address nonprofit issues in an MBA course on strategic management. A rewritten version of the course is likely to start from a discussion of stakeholders and the range of competitive and collaborative strategies rather than assuming a competitive market and that the only stakeholders that matter are shareholders.

Many faculty are sympathetic and responsive to the idea of thinking about the particular needs of nonprofit managers and have seen it as a way of enriching the curriculum of their courses and making them of wider relevance. For example, major case studies on nonprofits have been introduced into other MBA courses without our intervention. However, the implicit conceptual bias toward business in most management courses has been much harder to eliminate.

Second, our experience suggests that the question is as much how the concentration strategy is pursued as whether it is the appropriate strategy. The school attracts about one-third of its MBA students from the public sector and offers them an elective toward the end of that program. This has been a relatively *un*successful approach in terms of student numbers. This suggests that if a concentration is offered it should be at the start of a program, for both marketing and educational reasons.

The Debate about Academic Level

Should nonprofit programs be offered at the master's level or at the certificate level? Where can greater impact be achieved? What is the best use of limited faculty time? Again, the experience of the VSMP strongly confirms the decision to offer courses initially at the certificate level. Essentially, there are two reasons.

First, the way the program developed demonstrates that it is possible to offer a great deal to a wide range of students at what is nominally the certificate level. Such a program need not be uncritical and atheoretical, and it certainly need not be "beneath" those who already possess a degree. More than half of the students in the VSMP courses already possess a degree, and a significant minority possess two degrees. Some have been "refugees" from MBA programs they found meaningless. The course materials contain much that is intellectually demanding, and staff have yet to receive a complaint from students that it is too light, shallow, or easy. Nevertheless, the courses have also been successfully completed by many who left high school with no academic qualifications at all.

Second, a course at certificate level can address a much wider market, because such a course can offer a great deal to graduates and senior managers, while a master's level course offers much less to more junior staff and nongraduates. Moreover, at least in the U.K., master's level programs tend to be longer, more expensive, and more prone to "academic drift." Hence, they may often not be an appropriate commitment of scarce time and resources for those who are seeking a more serious and sustained form of management development than is available from short courses and reading the emerging professional literature.

This is, however, a hard message to put across in marketing the program. Many feel that only a master's qualification will enhance their employability. Personnel staff in particular, operating with a narrow "person-job fit" model of training, find it difficult to accept that a course can be hugely rewarding for people in such a wide range of circumstances.

The Wider Applicability of Distance Learning

There is no doubt about the general applicability or popularity of distance taught management courses. In the U.K. context this has been one of the fastest growing areas of management education over the last ten years. Indeed, the Open University Business School is by far the largest single provider of management education in the U.K. or Europe. Over 125,000 managers have taken courses since the school started in 1983.

The enrollment in VSMP courses also suggests that supported open learning can be popular among nonprofit managers. The enhanced accessibility of the courses adds to their attractiveness. There has been a study group in the Orkney Islands, and the courses have been studied by a wheelchair user living in a rural area for whom no other provision was realistic and by visually impaired students using a recorded version of the course. It also means that people can study part-time while they continue to work. This is an important issue in the voluntary sector, where many people work in small and medium-sized organizations, where it is difficult to spare staff.

Perhaps more fundamental, the challenge facing higher education is to find new and more cost-effective ways of meeting the ever-rising demands that a knowledge-based economy places on it. In such a context, the very different cost structure of distance learning has obvious attractions. For example, the underlying economies of scale mean that the only constraints the VSMP faces are on the marketing side; there are no practical limits to the number of students that the program can absorb while still maintaining a consistent quality. Indeed, if numbers were to double, the price of courses could be reduced. (The Open University social science foundation course has an intake of 12,000 students, which is greater than the entire student population of many conventional universities in the U.K.)

Nevertheless, the extent to which such an approach can be replicated elsewhere is far from clear. The initial investment cost is, by the standards of higher education, very substantial. Also, the Open University with its high-quality model of distance learning arose in very particular circumstances, and these have not been widely replicated elsewhere. In most other contexts, so far, distance learning is a way of extending at low cost the catchment for already existing courses by use of correspondence, telephone, satellite, or the Internet. Thus many of the costs may be hidden or spread over other programs. But the underlying model of higher education (where teaching is by individuals rather than the institution) remains the same, and the scale of operations remains fairly limited.

Hence, the question of the effectiveness and viability of distance learning in other contexts is complex and uncertain, not least because the underlying technologies continue to evolve rapidly.

The Marketing Challenge

Another major challenge, and one that was seriously underestimated at the start of the program, was to find effective ways to market the program. Some of these problems are internal; the others stem from the nature of the market. Internally, the VSMP does not really benefit from the main thrust of the OUBS marketing, which focuses on the school's main generic courses and is aimed primarily at the corporate sector. There was also concern that including the VSMP and other more specialized programs in the main marketing effort reduced its effectiveness; for example, the main school brochure was seen as being too complex. The solution has been to give the VSMP its own dedicated marketing resource. However, because the program only attracts relatively small numbers, securing adequate resources for this has required political effort and persistence.

The second set of problems relates to the market itself. The voluntary and non-profit sector in the U.K. is complex and fragmented. Various subsectors, such as housing associations, churches, and aid agencies, tend to have their own communication networks. A marketing strategy has to be quite complex and sophisticated to reach the different market segments. Another factor has been the sector's prevailing training culture, which has been very heavily geared towards one- or two-day training courses rather than sustained management development. The VSMP market research also identified important barriers: the relatively low training budgets in voluntary organizations, low incomes, and pressure on people's time. All of these stem from the pressure on resources within the sector and the desire to keep administrative costs to a minimum. We have been able to address this last problem in part by establishing a bursary fund. This is means-related and can partially cover the costs of taking courses in the program. To date, approximately 20 percent of students have received a bursary.

Finally, in promoting the program to larger organizations and federations, the VSMP has sometimes experienced the same difficulties as the OU Business School experiences in relation to the corporate sector: Many human resources and training personnel are reluctant to adopt a program that they cannot help shape and deliver. Personnel staff have frequently shown no interest and continued to arrange their own in-house training at far higher cost. It has been hard to avoid observing that they may have an economic interest in "make" rather than "buy."

A Business School Environment—Threat or Opportunity?

Cyert (1988, p. 49) has argued strongly that a business school is the wrong location for nonprofit management education, suggesting that "the evidence is strong that nonprofit management curricula become lost in a business school. . . . Perhaps the major reason is the education of the faculty. They have generally studied some aspect of the business firm, and their interests are attuned to the firm."

The experience of the Open University VSMP suggests that Cyert's conclusions are overly pessimistic if not plain wrong. It may be that the Open University is an unusual case. With a significant proportion of students from the public sector, OUBS faculty have been supportive of trying to broaden their courses to make better provision for students coming from nonprofit organizations. Many faculty have at least some experience of involvement in the voluntary sector that they can draw upon.

Operating within a business school context has several advantages. The program is able to offer a range of courses which would be difficult or expensive to provide independently. Students benefit from mixing with managers in other sectors, a benefit that grows as the boundaries between sectors become more blurred. Being in a business school also allows nonprofit managers to gain a general management qualification, which many desire.

Operating within a business school is not without problems. The majority of management textbooks draw on research or case studies based on large businesses. Even faculty sympathetic to the nonprofit sector are unaware of the difficulties of applying established business concepts to this area. This is exacerbated by the fact that a small core of specialist nonprofit management staff cannot easily make an input into a wide range of courses as well as support the concentration on nonprofit management.

However, in the VSMP's experience, the greatest challenges come in areas concerning the "commercial" aspects and marketing of the program. The OUBS is self-financing. The fees it charges for its courses are its revenue. In this context a concentration in nonprofit management is only a relatively small part of the business. This can lead to tensions. On the one hand, it is recognized that having the VSMP adds a distinctive dimension to the image of the school and enriches its curriculum. In addition, as many business and public sector leaders are involved with the nonprofit sector, having a strong presence in this area can benefit the school in other markets. On the other hand, when it comes to making commercial decisions, it is clear that the school can often make a better return on its money by investing in more "profitable" business courses. Because of these factors, when it comes to getting new staff for the program or establishing an adequate marketing budget, it has sometimes been necessary for program staff to "fight their corner" vigorously within the school. There is clearly a danger that the program could become. Staff are optimistic that this won't happen because of the other benefits the school derives and the support of many other faculty, but the ultimate test—how the program would be treated if the school faced serious financial difficulties—has not yet arisen.

CONCLUSIONS

A review of some nine years' work suggests that three points are likely to be of most interest for an international audience.

First, the VMSP experience described indicates that a substantial market for university-based and graduate-level management education can be created and that this will meet the requirements of those seeking a more serious and sustained treatment of management issues than is available through short, workshop-based training programs. However, for this to happen, faculty must conceive of their programs as contributions to continuous professional development and not as purely academic courses whose function is to enable students to discuss theories whose practical implications students must work out for themselves. Professional development implies supporting students in relating concepts to their own experience and extending their repertoire of skills and behaviors. Such courses should be rigorous, require theoretical content, and encourage critical and reflexive skills; it is of little benefit to the nonprofit sector simply to socialize its leaders in management-speak. Such professional development will be valued by a very wide range of people, from those with little formal education to those with a strong academic background, from those in senior positions in larger organizations to the single staff member.

Second, this case highlights the challenge of finding more cost-effective and widely accessible models of graduate level education. For both commercial and educational reasons, the education of nonprofit managers is problematic. Assuming a traditional model of higher education, nonprofit managers constitute too small and impoverished a group to excite much interest, and faculty lack the depth of understanding to teach them effectively. However, with supported distance learning and national recruitment, these limitations can be overcome; a significant demand can be created, and available expertise can be tapped. Students need no longer be marginal to other programs. How, and how far, this model can be adapted to the institutional circumstances in other countries remains unclear. But experience suggests that if economies of scales are to be achieved, they hinge on investments in two areas. The first is in materials development, to ensure that students work with clear and stimulating resources that provide a foundation for other activities and make the best use of their study time. The second is developing an elaborate infrastructure of roles, policies, and procedures to provide support to students through a mix of face-to-face, telephone, and computer-mediated forms of interaction and to develop adjunct faculty through induction, training support, and supervision to ensure consistency of standards and support.

Third, the VSMP experience throws important light on the scope for offering nonprofit "concentrations" within a business school environment. Given a sympathetic faculty, the balance of advantages and disadvantages clearly favors this strategy and location. Moreover, it appears that circumstances are shifting to favor this location even more strongly. As the blurring of boundaries between the sectors proceeds, as educational technologies for distance learning become more flexible, and as faculty understanding of and support for a nonprofit concentration increase, the position of the program becomes stronger educationally, economically, and politically within the institution. Indeed, it is now possible to envisage and discuss what might be called a "genuinely generic" management course, one in which a core of generic material is enhanced by additional resources for a wide range of different sectors and industries, including, but certainly not only, nonprofit organizations. Such a structure could then be further enhanced by computer conferencing that supports sector-specific networks of students and provides them with space for their own discussions. In broad terms, this is the model that is now being explored for the Open University MBA, which already attracts 30–40 nonprofit managers per year. This also emphasizes the fact that the VSMP is not a fixed offering but something that continues to evolve and expand.

5

Management Education for the Irish Voluntary Sector: First Steps in Program Design

Gemma Donnelly-Cox and Geoffrey MacKechnie

INTRODUCTION

This chapter documents the early stages in a program of research leading to a course in voluntary sector management. The origins of the program lie in the authors' view that the voluntary sector in Ireland is underserviced both as a subject of theoretical inquiry and in the provision of high-quality management education. We thought it would be possible to redress this situation through the careful design of a program of research and education targeted specifically at sector development. To this end, in 1995 we began to prepare a project to investigate the problems of managing effectively in the Irish voluntary sector. Although the School of Business Studies at Trinity College, Dublin, did not offer degree courses or other qualifications in nonprofit sector management,[1] some of its general management courses, in particular a taught master's degree in organizational behavior, were attracting small but consistent numbers of participants from the nonprofit sector. The authors investigated what nonprofit managers sought in the courses they had completed at Trinity. From this preliminary review, the authors gained some insight into management issues for the sector. This chapter reports on this early investigation and, in a postscript, on the subsequent developments since December 1996.

THE IRISH VOLUNTARY SECTOR

Ireland presents an interesting case history of the development of voluntary organizations. The country has a long-established and vibrant tradition of voluntary activity, which has thrived on informality and the largely unquestioning support of a generous giving public. However, in recent years, as greater emphasis has been placed on the rights of service recipients and the need for professionalism in voluntary agencies, concerns about a comparatively weak regulatory environment have emerged.

Ireland has a strong tradition of voluntary action. Political and social conditions have favored community-oriented nonprofit activity in the arts, sport, health, social welfare, and education domains. Religious influence has been credited with inculcating a sense of duty to be charitable and with underpinning a late twentieth century commitment to social justice, empowerment, and self-help (Ruddle and Donoghue, 1995, p. 13). The direct involvement of religious personnel in service delivery organizations has also been noted as significant within the sector.[2] Nonetheless, the role of religious personnel in the sector is thought to be declining because of a reduction in their numbers and also because of changing attitudes about the role of religion in Irish society.

Irish voluntary activity is also characterized by low formalization and lack of regulation. While the concept of a voluntary, "third" sector is understood and accepted, it is not delineated through an unambiguous definition of nonprofit organization or through charitable legislation. Ireland has no register of voluntary organizations, no register of charities, no supervision of entities that obtain charitable status, and no requirement in law that fundraising organizations make their accounts available for public inspection (Ruddle and Donoghue, 1995, p. 19). In this respect, Ireland presents a less rigorous regulatory environment than either Britain or the United States.

To a larger extent than in Britain, with whom much is shared, the voluntary tradition in Ireland has not been replaced by the public sector. The practice of the state has been to secure welfare provision through voluntary organizations, many of them church-run, instead of developing state welfare agencies. The result is that many areas of health and welfare provision have remained primarily in the voluntary sector.

There has been a tendency in Ireland to conceptualize the voluntary sector in terms of its "goodness," with a previous Minister for Social Welfare describing the sector as "the caring heart of society." Such popular conceptualizations of voluntary activity and the voluntary sector place great emphasis on ethos and little, if any, on how aspiration is best transformed into action. If we take the view that voluntary organizations are distinctive in terms of values, staffing, funding, and governance (O'Neill and Young, 1988), in Ireland there has been great emphasis on values but much less on the latter three elements. The preference for the term "voluntary" over "nonprofit" within the country may be consistent with the emphasis on ethos and values in popular conceptualizations.

Emerging Trends

While there is much continuity within the Irish voluntary sector, some of the distinctive practices that have developed are now being challenged as counterproductive to the aims of sector development. Trends toward formalization and clarification are emerging, mainly from larger organizations.[3] For example, there is increasing interest in more pervasive policing of organizational activity through state regulation. Increasingly, there is support for regulation of activities such as fundraising, where lack of clarity brings with it the potential for scandal.

Internal regulation is also an issue for many organizations within the sector. Managers are attending courses and reading books that emphasize that voluntary organizations should become "more professional" and demonstrate "effective management." Service providers should be able to offer a full range of quality services to their client groups and run their agencies effectively. Organizations are subject to requirements of increased accountability to stakeholders, particularly clients and funders.

As the emphasis on professionalism and regulation of the sector has grown, individuals attempting to promote these issues within the sector have discovered that there are few mechanisms for fostering a sectoral identity within the country. Efforts to pursue sectoral interests have been frustrated by the inability of organizations to work effectively together. Organizations have been unable to agree on a focus for joint action and have been further hampered by the paucity of shared language and views on critical issues. A key consequence of this "sector fragmentation" is that those who would attempt to represent sectoral interests find that they can make little impact on the state decision-making processes. The inability of the sector to make its case to government is matched by the state's poor record for actively involving the sector in consultation processes:

Despite government pronouncements on the importance of voluntary activity . . . the approach to the development of the voluntary sector in the Republic of Ireland has been criticized as being largely piecemeal and tentative. . . . Recent reports have been critical of the treatment of voluntary organizations by government, maintaining that they are largely taken for granted and highlighting the lack of an agreed framework for involving the sector in consultation and planning. (Gaskin and Davis Smith, 1995, p. 12)

The characteristics and trends just identified indicate that Irish voluntary organizations are facing an increasingly challenging operating environment. Many sector managers are committed to increased professionalization and regulation but have not established how they will work together to pursue these issues of mutual concern. The skills and expertise necessary to respond and act within their changing environment differ from those needed for operational efficiency.

The Current Supply of Management Education

Within Ireland, there is demand for provision of management education and training from voluntary organizations, from the umbrella bodies[4] that represent them, and from individuals working or wishing to work within the sector. The responses to this demand have included short training courses, courses of one year or more that award a certificate or diploma, graduate courses for particular subsectors, and distance learning courses. The variety of courses, though not all available courses, is summarized in Table 5.1.

Table 5.1 indicates that there is a range of targeted programs available in Ireland. None of these, however, addresses the strategic role of nonprofit management for interpreting and acting on external information. Further, there are few opportunities for practitioners to access a forum in which they might consider common identity and joint action. Indeed, the more senior the course participants, the more stratified the course in terms of orientation toward subsectors such as the arts or health.

Table 5.1
Range of Voluntary Sector Management Courses in Ireland

Sample Course Type	Sample Institutions[a]	Course Length	Selectivity of Entry	Level of Participant	Qualification/Accreditation
Short training course	National Social Service Board	One- and two-day seminars	Must be from a voluntary org.	Any org. member	None
	Carmichael Center[b] for Voluntary Organizations	From half a day up to 10 half days	Must be from a voluntary org.	Any org. member	Certificate of attendance
Certificate/ diploma course in voluntary sector management	Dublin City University	One year, eight hours per week	Selective	Some managerial experience	Certificate[c]
	National College of Industrial Relations	One year, two hours per week	Open entry	Open to all participants	Certificate
	Open University	Distance learning course	Open entry	Open to all participants	Diploma
Graduate, sector-specific courses at diploma or master's level	University College Dublin	One year full-time	Selective	Graduate of an under-graduate degree course	Graduate Diploma in Arts Administration
	Royal College of Surgeons in Ireland	Two years part-time	Selective	Doctors, nurses, and medical administrators	MBA for Health-care Professionals

a. With the exception of the Open University distance learning program, all the cited courses are offered in Dublin.

b. The Carmichael Center is an "incubator" for small voluntary organizations that are not in a position to establish their own premises and/or facilities. The center runs short courses for its member organizations and external bodies.

c. A certificate is a nondegree award that indicates the student has been examined in the course subject matter and has passed the examinations. Certificate courses are sometimes accredited by the National Council for Educational Awards, which increases the attractiveness of the course for potential participants.

We are not convinced that there is a strong sense of what is needed in a program of education for managers in voluntary organizations. There has been no formal polling of the market to assess needs and wants. This contrasts with the approach adopted in Britain, where, for example, Cranfield, the London School of Economics, and the Open University have made concerted efforts to assess sector needs (Harris, 1991). Up to the present, Irish business schools have rarely been responsive to suggestions that they could offer qualifications targeted to meet the needs of this sector.

ISSUES RELEVANT TO COURSE DESIGN

Our first step in investigating whether the School of Business Studies should offer management education for the voluntary sector was to contact the senior members of voluntary organizations who had taken a Trinity graduate management development course. In our initial discussions with course participants, we heard much about the rapid change in the operating environment of voluntary organizations and the increasing demand for management skills. We then decided to interview several of them to find out what they had gained from the course.

We interviewed 10 senior executives who had taken our MSc[5] in Organizational Behavior between 1985 and 1995 to identify what it is about the course that attracts these participants and what they feel they gain from it. This master's course, run in conjunction with the Irish Management Institute, is designed for executives who are interested in developing their capacity for "people management." The program commences every second year and runs for two years on a part-time basis. Most participants are sponsored by their organizations. The average class size is 25, with between three and five of the participants coming from the voluntary sector.[6]

We also run MSc programs in business administration, management practice, and public sector management, and we run a one-year, full-time MBA. None of these programs has attracted participation from the voluntary sector with the same constancy as the MSc in Organizational Behavior.[7]

When we interviewed the past participants, we asked them why they took the MSc course, what they found useful, and what was of lesser relevance. We then asked them how the course could have been improved for their own purposes. Finally, we sought their views on a targeted, voluntary sector course with distinctive content and curriculum. On initial analysis, we noted considerable diversity in the answers to these questions, leading us to consider O'Neill and Young's comments on the disparate nature of sector organizations: "[T]here is no such thing as the prototypical nonprofit organization. . . . Thus, a key question in the development of nonprofit management education is whether, as has apparently been decided in the other sectors, nonprofits have enough in common to justify and encourage a distinct, unitary management education tradition of their own" (O'Neill and Young, 1988, p. 11). However, there were also several points of convergence across a range of issues raised by the course participants, relating both to managing effectively in the sector and to management education. Their views, when considered in conjunction with the experiences related in the literature (O'Neill and Young, 1988) and our own experience in designing and offering MSc courses, have aided us in developing some preliminary views that may be relevant for effective course design. From these, we have derived a set of five issues of relevance for course design and delivery. Underlying these issues is our view that ultimately, given the particular characteristics of the Irish sector, we should work from first principles on program design. We anticipate this will assist us in avoiding unrealistic assumptions about the needs of the sector and inappropriate content for the resulting course(s) of education. We present the five issues following as preliminary considerations.

Should the Course be Exclusive to the Voluntary Sector?

Various commentators have warned that voluntary organization managers can get "lost" in a group of mainly for-profit organization managers and that some measure of protection might be needed to safeguard their interests (Cyert, 1988). One of our MSc course participants mirrored this view. She felt the course was too weighted toward the corporate participant. The predominance of large organizations in the course reinforced a commercial ethos alien to voluntary organizations and detrimental to the understanding of their outlook. Tunnel vision could develop among these participants, creating barriers to understanding other perspectives.

Our initial assumption was that we should focus on developing targeted courses exclusive to the voluntary sector. However, we found in our discussions with past students that all of them, including the respondent who was critical of the mix on her course, argued for a cross-sectoral mix of participants. They liked the fact that the course brought together people from different backgrounds. For those who only had experience of one organization or one sector, this was particularly valuable. The diversity was a "broadening experience," offering opportunities for networking.

Opportunities for networking outside the sector were rated very highly by several of the senior executives. A mixed course such as the MSc in Organizational Behavior provides a rare forum for information exchange and raises a query about the value of segregating sectors for the purposes of management education. O'Neill and Young (1988, p. 12) have observed "patterns of interconnection" in the United States and have noted "perhaps managers from all sectors ought to be educated under the one roof."

For persons with a strong professional but limited managerial background, exposure to "professional managers" provided "a jump-start." As one health care manager with a nursing background commented, "I was exposed to real managers with motivations very different from my own. It helped me move from a patient to an operational focus."

Several participants commented that the diversity of course participants helped them to recognize the demands of their own roles. One noted that it was a pleasure to learn that commercial management was often less challenging than running her organization. Her environment of huge budgets yet scarce resources, hundreds of staff, 24-hour operation, high uncertainty, and "ferocious unpredictability" made the management of a manufacturing operation look simple in comparison.

As there is currently no forum for communication across the voluntary sector, we suspect that some of the reticence expressed regarding a "sector course" reflects lack of experience with a wider variety of organizations from different subsectors. Of course, the interest in diversity expressed by MSc participants may simply reflect the leanings of a small sample who had initially chosen a business-oriented course. In parallel, we need to investigate whether the issue reflects an underlying sector need for exposure to broader management concepts and contexts, as this would need to be addressed in the design of course content.

Specific Participants

Our MSc programs are differentiated and tailored to a narrower constituency than, for example, our MBA. Participation is limited to individuals with sufficient experience to apply the course material to their own work situations. The teaching pattern is also varied to accommodate their work schedules. Our initial views on a course for the sector would be that we would target senior managers in voluntary organizations, mirroring the MSc constituency.

Views on the degree to which the course should be targeted and tailored were mixed when we spoke with previous course participants. Some said they needed targeted material, but not necessarily a targeted course. One suggested additional modules or tag-on workshops in a program such as the MSc in Organizational Behavior. One woman commented that while the course suited her and her organization, there were many, mainly smaller voluntary organizations in which management skills were "extremely underdeveloped or simply not developed." She felt they required targeted courses that would focus exclusively on their development needs.

Past participants of the MSc have consistently lauded the diversity of the class. They say they enjoyed the mix of private and voluntary organizations and felt they all gained from it. Diversity was "an eye opener"; too narrow a mix risked becoming "too incestuous." We need to explore whether the cross-sectoral representation was as important as the variety of organizations represented. Would, for example, a priest find a mix of relief organization, hospital, and school managers as stimulating as bankers and manufacturing managers?

Initially, we find the value placed on diversity a very relevant factor for course design. The challenge would appear to be one of maintaining diversity among participants, yet identifying significant and relevant common factors for which a distinctive body of material can be identified (Butler and Collins, 1995). This issue has been faced in designing other targeted courses—for example, our MSc for public sector managers.

One valuable piece of information we have learned from former course participants is that there is no forum for senior personnel within the Irish voluntary sector to gather and exchange ideas. While course participants saw the MSc course as a vehicle for networking with managers outside their sector, they were conscious that they had few organized opportunities to do the same within the sector.

Organizational roles of participants also need to be considered. Voluntary organization managers who have taken the MSc course have tended to be people with professional qualifications but without a grounding in principles of management. One of the concerns which has been raised about generic management education is that it does not cater to the professional side of nonprofit management, and that graduates of these programs are unable to evaluate the technical competence of organizational professionals (Slavin, 1988). It is our expectation that many of our potential participants will be professionals who have been promoted into managerial positions because they are good at teaching, nursing, or ministering. They will be looking for the generic management skills which will allow them to make operational decisions outside their areas of professional competence.

Course Content

Is there a body of knowledge specific to the voluntary sector? North American course designers have noted the absence of a body of knowledge (O'Neill and Young, 1988). Conceivably, as Ireland lacks formalized definitions of organization or sector and as thinking on the voluntary organization as a particular organizational form is poorly developed, identification of a body of knowledge for the sector would pose great difficulty. This affects the development of curriculum. If a body of knowledge cannot be identified, on what basis should a curriculum be designed? O'Neill and Young (1988, p. 18) have suggested that "the characteristics of nonprofit organizations and the characteristics of nonprofit organization management must be the dominant force shaping any curriculum to meet the needs of these managers."

When we spoke with former students of the MSc program, they presented great variety in their ranking of "best" or "most important" curriculum content. The favored material tended to relate to the particular demands of their job. For example, the matron of a large maternity hospital favored the industrial relations and human resource management content, followed closely by seminars on organizational politics. The provincial of a religious order revelled in strategic planning and was remembered by his classmates for the way he brought Porter's five forces model alive. The financial director of a hospital run by a religious order remembered how the sessions on organization development and change management helped him make a significant contribution to an organizational renewal program. The chief executive of a women's center emphasized the content on leadership, which she viewed to be sadly lacking in the women's movement in Ireland. All were able to suggest other material that should be found in a voluntary organization management program.

The views on content related more specifically to voluntary organization management were mixed. Some were disappointed that lecturers made no attempt to apply the course content to voluntary organization cases. They felt that the lecturers were "playing to the mainly business crowd—they didn't really know anything about the needs that voluntary organizations address." Others specifically stated that they didn't want "voluntary organization content." One participant reasoned that "the systems [in her organization] are the same, only harder. I know about the sector from twenty years of working in it.[8] I want the course to tell me about the hard stuff, not the sector." Her focus was on the body of management literature, not the context in which it was to be applied.

In contrast to the preceding perspective, one respondent objected to the style of course content presentation, on the basis that its delivery style was one of "someone coming to fill empty vessels." He felt this to be completely at odds with the process orientation of his workplace, where what happened was a negotiated process agreed to by all participants. In presenting a body of knowledge, he felt, lecturers were denying participants the opportunity to select material related to and based on their own experience. The situation was reinforced by lecturers tending to "deliver for up to two thirds of the time . . . leaving perhaps only one third for discussion and student participation."

Students were also able to identify additional content that they thought would be relevant to voluntary organization managers. They suggested business law, finance (mainly management accounting), and employment legislation as topics to receive more thorough treatment. These elements would assist them in interpreting the information they were presented within their own organizations.

Students had mixed experiences of transferring the course material into the workplace. Responses varied from examples of specific situations in which the content was useful through to a sense of individual outlooks being altered by course attendance, therefore affecting the way the participant would respond to work situations. Only one of the respondents found himself facing an institutional barrier to his learning in the workplace. He noted that "When I came back, nobody was interested that I came back developed." He attributed this to a poor identification process for training needs in his organization.

A weakness in course content is the lack of systematic understanding of voluntary sector management and organization in Ireland. Without this, it is difficult to ascertain what material is generally relevant—regardless of the sector—and whether there is sector-specific course content to be included. As O'Neill and Young (1988, p. 13) have commented, "the preferred education program for nonprofit managers is an empirical matter which should derive from detailed study of what these managers actually do." Our preliminary discussions with past course participants have convinced us that the long-term utility of any course is dependent upon such an understanding.

Opposition to Managerialism

Underlying our investigation is the assumption that managers in the voluntary sector are in favor of education programs. We have noted the forces for increased professionalism and the emphasis placed on effectiveness by evaluation processes. However, we have not considered whether antipathy to management and therefore management education may exist. In the U.K., increased emphasis on management education and sector professionalism has raised concerns about "creeping managerialism" and fears that too great an emphasis is placed on being "business-like."[9] While, in itself, the emphasis on education and professionalism would appear to be a laudable objective, it has been argued that the emphasis can upset the value placed on volunteering.

When we spoke with course participants, they suggested a number of problems that could arise in designing courses for the sector. It was noted that an antipathy to "things managerial" exists in many Irish voluntary organizations. Linked to this is the tendency in many organizations to find leadership a "difficult concept." In these organizations, management and leadership are viewed as contradicting an organizational emphasis on consensus, process, and the full integrity of all members.

One participant argued that if a course were to be designed for voluntary organizations exclusively, attention would have to be paid to the "learning, training culture of these organizations. There is a constant process of negotiating with people, establishing contracts with them. They would expect a course to be run in the same way. Everything should be open to review." He felt that within his own organization, any attempt by a manager to stand outside this process would be viewed as being at odds with the ethos of the organization.

Can ethos and an emphasis on management be construed as opposite values? It would appear that within some organizations, this has become the case. An illustrative example was provided in the differing perceptions of the organization and the value of education held by the chief executive and a junior staff member of a large health organization. The chief executive was a participant in the Trinity MSc program. She argued for taking "real" management courses that exposed her to a "wider vision of the world." She was vehement in her objection to a targeted course, as she believed it would become too focused on organizational ethos. "Ethos belongs in your organization, not in a course. The course should show you the world, not your own navel." Her view contrasted strongly with that of the junior staff member, who was at that time enrolled in a targeted certificate course in management offered at a Dublin college. It was his view that senior executives were out of touch with the reality of his organization as he saw it. "They treat [it] like a business . . . they have no idea of why we work here or what the clients think of the service." From his perspective, management education has to be concerned with ethos and the distinctiveness of the voluntary organization.

Our preliminary investigation has indicated that we need to consider further the relationship between ethos and organizational practices. We need to gain an understanding of what makes voluntary organizations distinctive and how this may impinge upon the delivery of effective management education.

Relationship with Existing Institutions

A final issue that we wish to raise has not originated from our discussion with past MSc students but rather from our own experience—and that offered by persons from other institutions—of initiating courses within a university environment. The best content in the world does not guarantee the success of a course. A good project without an internal champion can face daunting hurdles as the proposal works its way through the approval process. Some universities are more willing to allow experimentation in course design than others. Therefore, issues in course design include piloting the proposed course through the approval process within the university and establishing its credibility with the potential participants.

Keane and Merget (1988), in reflecting on their own program at George Washington University, suggested co-opting professionals through an advisory board.[10] One of the espoused benefits of this practice is the legitimacy it lends to the proposed new course and the program once approved. Additionally, depending on the composition of the board, it may signal to the constituency that the university is seeking to involve the sector in the design and delivery of the course. If an interest is taken in the program through an advisory board, the potential for course participants to transfer knowledge and skills from the classroom to the organizational setting is thought to be increased.[11]

It could also be argued that the appointment of an advisory board has its price. Course designers might be obliged to accept the advice of persons who do not necessarily have a helpful vision of what should be learned. Practitioners may well be conservative and anxious to preserve their hegemony. As Disraeli put it: "A practical man is a man who can be relied upon to repeat the mistakes of his ancestors." Course designers should therefore think carefully about what they hope to achieve from putting supporting structures in place and consider the potential consequences, both positive and negative.

FIRST STEPS IN PROGRAM DESIGN

Our discussions with the MSc students and the five issues we have presented have provided us with a departure point for developing an understanding of sector needs and also for broaching the question of targeted education. Moving forward from this preliminary work, we have secured funding for a two-year research program to undertake a more systematic study. Our objective is to gather from a representative range of voluntary organizations firsthand accounts of their strengths and weaknesses in coping effectively with changing circumstances. Methodologically, we have a choice between selecting a wide but shallow sample or opting to study fewer cases in greater depth. Our review of the current literature has led us to conclude that the theory of effectiveness in the sector is not sufficiently developed for a broad survey of the field in Ireland. At this stage, we intend to concentrate on developing 15 to 20 analytical case studies. We plan to derive case studies that will illustrate the skills and problems relevant to the sector. Our two-year project allows for six months of preparation, one year to 14 months of data gathering, and four to six months of data analysis and case writing. At the end of the two-year period, we plan to host a conference at Trinity that will bring together interested members of the academic community and practitioners from Irish voluntary organizations, in particular from the case study organizations.

Our opening position is that we need to know what it is that constitutes management effectiveness within the sector before we can design a program of management education. Much of the work conducted in the voluntary and nonprofit sectors abroad focuses on developing measures of organizational effectiveness (Herman and Heimovics, 1994; Kanter and Summers, 1987; Osborne and Tricker, 1995), often in response to the growing requirement that organizations be evaluated on their effectiveness in utilizing grants, running contracts, and delivering services (Murray and Tassie, 1994). There has been little work carried out to examine managerial and organizational effectiveness in the Irish voluntary sector, beyond one study of managerial competencies in the arts (Clancy, 1995). While we do not wish to reinvent the wheel, we hypothesize that the available literatures are useful but not necessarily transferable in their entirety to the "Irish case."

Regardless of the outcomes in terms of course design, it is our intention that our two-year research project make a significant contribution to what is known about Irish voluntary organizations. It is our expectation, however, that this knowledge will be of assistance in identifying the challenges facing these organizations and the most effective ways for their managers to deal with them.

As our objectives for the project have developed, we are moving towards an overall goal of a center that would provide a focus for research and education. At the completion of the research project, we hope to have a firm foundation for the development of a center in which research can be undertaken and skills for management effectiveness in voluntary organizations can be developed.

Our immediate objective at the conclusion of the project will be dissemination of the research results. We hope to provide a clearer picture of the sector through our in-depth focus on individual organizations and the changes being experienced. Ideally, we will be able to design appropriate programs of education and develop a further research agenda. Overall, we hope that success in the project will help us to generate wider interest in the management requirements of the voluntary sector and attract support for the center.

POSTSCRIPT

Since presenting our initial findings and aspirations in Berkeley in March 1996, the School of Business Studies has consolidated a core group of staff and research students with an interest in researching and teaching in the area of nonprofit sector management.[12] Additionally, we have been approached by individuals, funding agencies, and umbrella organizations with an interest in Trinity carrying out work in the areas of management education provision and sector research. In December 1996, the authors were joined by a full-time research assistant, Andrew O'Regan, and our two-year study of management in Irish nonprofit organizations commenced. Our present aspiration is that the study will lead to a master's program for nonprofit sector managers that, it is hoped, will reflect a deeper understanding of the Irish sector and its management challenges than is currently possible.

Our project commenced with a focus on sector mapping, based on a broad literature survey and interviews with senior managers in Irish voluntary organizations.[13] As we moved on to the case study phase of the project, we selected a group of 18 organizations that we will follow over a 12-month period, with a focus in each case on a particular management issue agreed upon between ourselves and the participating organizations. As of August 1997, we have secured the agreement of 17 of these organizations for participation in the project.

During the period we have worked on the project, a number of factors have contributed to renewed emphasis on the sector in Irish society. The Minister for Social Welfare, in consultation with the Department of Health, published a Green Paper on the sector in May 1997 (Department of Social Welfare, 1997). While not the level of commitment initially promised—a charter for voluntary services in the form of a White Paper has been expected since the 1970s—it is a positive step towards defining and legitimizing the role of the sector in Irish society. The sector has also benefited from the interest and support of the President of Ireland, Mary Robinson. President Robinson focused attention on the sector during her term of office and emphasized its function within society. However, the sector continues to lack an integral unifying focus; and when problems within particular organizations raise questions in the public mind about the sector as a whole, there is no mechanism by which the sector can respond with a single voice.[14]

The issues we identified following interviews with past MSc students have provided guidance in designing our research program. With regard to specific course participants, we have directed the emphasis of our research project towards organizational effectiveness and strategic leadership. We are focusing on personnel holding professional or managerial positions within voluntary organizations. At the same time, we have an opportunity to examine issues relating to organizational diversity through an innovative element of program design we have built into the project. We are running a chief executive seminar for the participating organizations between January and June 1998. The focus for each of the seminars will be drawn from the issues identified in the research project and will give us some feedback on how common issues are perceived by participants from across the sector. The decision to run the chief executive seminars for a group of very diverse organizations is in part tied to the feedback received from MSc students concerning the current lack of networking opportunities for sector managers.

Our experience with chief executives from diverse organizations may give us some guidance as to the value of a center for the sector. We currently propose that a center could facilitate the development of a sector forum, first through courses themselves and then through more targeted efforts to create a mechanism for exchange.

As our research program is focused on organization and management issues, we expect it will inform the development of a curriculum for a master's course. The case studies might become a key element of the course, assisting students in drawing links between generic management principles and models and their application in particular organizational settings. Successful curriculum development will depend on our ability to identify the issues relevant to management effectiveness and then to present principles and techniques that students can apply to their own situations. With sufficient coordination among course, manager, and organization, the curriculum could provide the foundation for action learning.

As of August 1997, our research program is progressing as planned. We have been gratified by the interest and enthusiasm of our participating case organizations and their general willingness to work with us on core management issues. Ideally, in December 1998 we will be in a strong position to report on the outcomes of the project and to announce the foundation of an Irish center for voluntary sector research and management education.

NOTES

1.   As of August 1997, this is still the position of the School.

2.   A regional study of service delivery organizations noted that almost two-thirds of voluntary organizations studied had religious involvement including founding the organization, providing direct financial aid, providing premises, and acting as director (Faughnan and Kelleher, 1993).

3.   There are exceptions, particularly among organizations that have managed extremely well without the encumbrances of state regulation and are therefore unenthusiastic about any change in the operating environment.

4.   Umbrella bodies are representative organizations with a membership of organizations. They may represent the interests of a particular subgroup, such as disability organizations (Disability Federation of Ireland), or of a particular issue common to organizations across a range of subgroups—for example, Focus on Children, which deals with children's issues for a wide range of organizations with separate agendas.

5.   In the School of Business Studies, an MSc degree is a two-year master's degree earned through coursework and research. MSc students take courses for one year, then write a thesis in the second year.

6.   Most of our voluntary sector participants have come from the areas of youth, health, social services, and religious life.

7.   Our MBA program is an intensive one-year program composed of core courses and a group project. It does attract managers from the voluntary sector, but it is unlikely to be the "course of first choice" for large numbers of practitioners. The other MSc courses are as ac-

cessible as the MSc in Organizational Behavior in terms of being part-time and run over two years, but they do not prove nearly as attractive to voluntary sector managers.

8.   Again, we suspect that her views reflect much experience of a particular subsector but little of the sector as a whole.

9.   This perspective has been offered by the National Center for Volunteering (formerly the Volunteer Center U.K.), a London-based organization that acts as a research, training, and information center on volunteering.

10.   In 1988, Keane and Merget offered a series of suggestions for course design and for ensuring the viability of a course for nonprofit management in a university setting. It is somewhat ironic that the course at George Washington University is one of the U.S. university programs that has not survived.

11.   One of our former MSc students reported that his organization had no interest in his attending the course and resisted his attempts to transfer course-generated learning into his workplace.

12.   The "Nonprofit Management Education 1996: A U.S. and World Perspective" conference, March 14–16, 1996, Berkeley, California, hosted by the University of San Francisco.

13.   In May 1997 we presented a paper to an Irish symposium of voluntary sector research, proposing a model for investigating managerial issues within a sector framework (O'Regan, Donnelly-Cox, and MacKechnie, 1997).

14.   Current examples include sex abuse cases involving Catholic priests and accusations of fundraising impropriety in an overseas aid organization.

Part 2

Special Issues

6

Nonprofit Management Education: Recommendations Drawn from Three Stakeholder Groups

Mary Tschirhart

Having specialized programs and courses for students of nonprofit management makes sense (Van Til and Hegyesi, 1996; NASPAA, 1992; Rubin, Adamski, and Block, 1989; Goldstein, 1989; Slavin, 1988). Managers of nonprofit organizations are likely to have missions to serve multiple stakeholders with potentially conflicting needs and expectations (Hodgkin, 1993) and to have diverse revenue streams that create complex strategic and operational challenges (Oster, 1995; Grønbjerg, 1993). Nonprofit organizations may be subject to different laws and reporting requirements than business or government agencies (Fishman and Schwarz, 1995), and their leadership may more often depend on a coalition of actors than on a single administrator (Drucker, 1990). Sophisticated methods for evaluating effectiveness are needed more in nonprofit organizations than in businesses, because of their greater demands for accountability, coupled with relatively intangible outcomes (Hodgkin, 1993; Kanter and Summers, 1987).

Despite these and other distinctions between nonprofits and other types of organizations, there is still much diversity within the nonprofit sector. Because of this diversity, no nonprofit management education program can hope to cover all aspects of the field (Van Til and Hegyesi, 1996). Resource constraints and the breadth of skills and knowledge relevant to management require tradeoffs in program offerings. Therefore, priorities need to be established in designing a nonprofit management education program. Understanding the perceived needs and practices of key stakeholders can help in determining these priorities. This chapter describes one school's study used to help set priorities and the general recommendations that can be drawn from the study for other providers of nonprofit management education.

THE INDIANA UNIVERSITY IN BLOOMINGTON EXPERIENCE

The School of Public and Environmental Affairs (SPEA) at Indiana University in Bloomington recently added a concentration in nonprofit management to its Master of Public Affairs program and a certificate program in nonprofit management for non-SPEA graduate students. The core requirements for the MPA degree provide a strong management and policy base. The concentration offers students the opportunity to develop and extend this base through nonprofit applications. The majority of courses in the concentration address the unique features and practices of nonprofit organizations and policies affecting them. Supplementary courses in the concentration offer generic management techniques helpful to nonprofit managers. The certificate is designed for graduate students pursuing degrees outside SPEA and nondegree students. Certificate students take three required courses (nonprofit management, financial management for nonprofits, and human resource management for nonprofits) and two electives chosen from a wide range of offerings.

To help in the development of the concentration and certificate, data were collected from three types of stakeholders: nonprofit managers, students planning careers as managers of nonprofit organizations, and faculty who taught a course covering an aspect of nonprofit management. Findings from the study suggested topics to be covered in required and elective courses, new formats for course delivery, strategies for promoting the programs, and the support of educational opportunities outside the classroom.

DESIGN OF THE STUDY

The study uses data collected in surveys of managers, students, and faculty. The data were collected in 1996, except for a second collection in early 1997 to augment the sample of students. Survey respondents evaluated the importance of 32 knowledge and skill areas that might be taught as part of a nonprofit management program. Students rated the importance of the areas to their careers as nonprofit managers, and faculty indicated their importance to students practicing or planning nonprofit management careers. Managers rated the importance of the areas to *any* nonprofit manager. The managers also reported their personal educational interests, barriers to pursuing education, desirable backgrounds for applicants for nonprofit positions, and personal and organizational characteristics. In addition, the managers and students indicated their use of a variety of educational resources.

The list of skill and knowledge areas was developed by the author, three nonprofit managers, and a doctoral student, using articles and reports identifying positive characteristics for nonprofit managers (Hoefer, 1993a, 1993b; Winter Commission, 1993; Non-Profit Program, 1992; NASPAA, 1992; Wish, 1991; and Rubin, Adamski, and Block, 1989). The labels for the areas were constructed to be as nonoverlapping and clear as possible, while remaining comprehensive but not overwhelming as a set. The list of areas was not expected to represent specific course titles. Rather, the list offered skill and knowledge areas that might be developed as a segment of a course or a complete course.

Samples

Nonprofit Managers. Ninety surveys were mailed to executive directors or designated contact persons using a city directory of the private nonprofit organizations in Bloomington. The directory excludes new grassroots organizations with no paid staff or budget, Greek fraternal organizations, churches and other places of worship, nonprofits legally affiliated with Indiana University, and chapters of professional membership associations. The directory attempts to capture all other types of nonprofits. Fifty-three managers returned surveys, a response rate of 59 percent. Most of the respondents hold the top administrative position in their organizations (71 percent), and all are managers. They have from one to 30 years of experience in the nonprofit sector, with an average of 12 years. Most (63 percent) have an undergraduate degree, and half (51 percent) have a graduate degree. The most common degrees are arts or humanities (16 percent), education (16 percent), social services (14 percent), and public administration (14 percent). Two of the respondents have business degrees, and one has a nonprofit management degree.

The managers in the sample represent a range of nonprofit organizations. The median staff size is nine; the mean is 37. The volunteer staff outnumber the paid professional staff in 61 percent of the organizations. Nine percent of the organizations do not use volunteers. Half (50 percent) have revenues of more than $300,000, with 34 percent having revenues of $100,000–$300,000 and 16 percent having revenues of less than $75,000. Service areas include arts, social services, mental and physical health, recreation, youth services, economic development, education, human rights, and environmental protection. Over half of the organizations (55 percent) are members of an association.

Students Pursuing Nonprofit Management Careers. Departments and schools at Indiana University in Bloomington with graduate students likely to have career interests in nonprofit organizations were blanketed with surveys. It is hard to calculate a response rate, as secretaries were relied on to see that surveys were distributed and sometimes stacks of surveys were simply left in student lounges. Seventy-three surveys were returned, with only 35 coming from students reporting that their first choice was to work in a nonprofit organization. To increase the sample of students, surveys were distributed to new graduate students in the School of Public and Environmental Affairs (SPEA) and students in a fund development course. This increased the final sample to 54. Only surveys from student respondents whose first choice was to have a management career in the nonprofit sector were used in the study. Students in the SPEA MPA program comprise 50 percent of the sample. The remainder of the sample is comprised of students in arts administration (20 percent); education (13 percent); business (9 percent); library and information science (6 percent); and health, physical education, and recreation (2 percent). Other schools or departments that might have students interested in nonprofit management careers, such as nursing and social work, are not represented in the sample because their programs are in Indianapolis and we wished to uncover the views and practices of Bloomington-based students.

Faculty Teaching about Nonprofits. Sixty-one Bloomington faculty members were sent surveys. The mailing included all Bloomington professors who are members of the Philanthropic Studies Faculty (a multidisciplinary group interested in nonprofits and affiliated with the Center on Philanthropy) or who had delivered a course over the last five years that appeared to be related to nonprofit management. Thirty-one surveys were returned, a 51 percent response rate, but only 24 of the surveys were from faculty members who believed they taught a course related to nonprofit management and who answered the questions. The 24 faculty members include six professors from the College of Arts and Sciences; five from the School of Health, Physical Education, and Recreation; four from the School of Education; three from the School of Public and Environmental Affairs; two from the School of Business; one from a research center; and one each from the schools of Law, Journalism, and Library and Information Sciences.

ANALYSES, FINDINGS, AND RECOMMENDATIONS

Importance of the Skill and Knowledge Areas to Any Nonprofit Manager

The Managers' Views of the Importance of the Areas. Table 6.1 summarizes the managers' views of the importance of the skill and knowledge areas to any nonprofit manager. It also provides correlations of the ratings with characteristics of the respondents' organizations. The areas are listed in order of their perceived importance. The eight areas rated, on average, as "very important" to any nonprofit manager are leadership, ethics and values in nonprofits, long-term planning, financial management, conducting effective meetings, creativity, public relations, and interpersonal skills. The managers see most of the other areas as important to any nonprofit manager. The only area falling below the midpoint of the importance scale is history of philanthropy and nonprofits.

The respondents' management experience may be reflected in their responses. If so, we have an indirect way of seeing whether managers are reporting that different types of nonprofits need different types of managers. Because of data limitations, we could only compare the organizations with small revenues (less than $300,000) to those with larger revenues (more than $300,000). No analyses using this measure of revenues produced significant results. The service type of an organization is likely to influence responses. However, the sample composition and size did not allow any useful contrasts based on service type. We looked in depth at two types of organizational characteristics: dependence on volunteers and size of professional staff.

We defined a volunteer-based organization as one in which the number of volunteers is greater than the number of paid professional staff members. Managers of volunteer-based organizations rate volunteer management significantly higher than do other managers. Managers of volunteer organizations rate managing change, legal issues for nonprofits, and policy advocacy and lobbying lower than do managers with less reliance on volunteers. Since volunteer organizations are typically less institutionalized, these managers may have fewer long-term staff members and long-established routines that encourage resistance to change. Legal knowledge may be rated as less important in volunteer-based organizations because fewer of these organizations are required to file legal documents related to taxes and personnel.

The number of paid professional staff members also influences some of the ratings. Managers of organizations with larger professional staffs rate Total Quality Management (TQM) and legal issues for nonprofits higher in importance than managers with smaller professional staffs. The managers with larger staffs rate fund-

Table 6.1
Managers' Ratings of Areas and Correlations of Areas with Organizational Characteristics

Skill and Knowledge Areas	Importance to Any Nonprofit Manager		Volunteer Based Organization	No. of Professional Paid Staff ($N = 53$)
	Mean	Std. Dev.	Correlation[1]	Correlation
Leadership	4.85	.36	-.058	.009
Ethics and values in nonprofits	4.79	.41	.151	-.080
Long-term planning	4.64	.53	-.236	.057
Financial management	4.58	.89	-.134	-.074
Conducting effective meetings	4.57	.61	-.032	.148
Creativity	4.54	.67	-.128	-.018
Public relations	4.54	.73	-.027	.079
Interpersonal skills	4.50	.67	-.041	-.063
Short-term planning	4.46	.78	.026	.149
Managing change	4.42	.78	-.398**	.181
Conflict management	4.28	.80	.076	-.141
Program evaluation	4.25	.79	-.072	-.048
Collaboration and networking	4.25	.95	-.134	-.213
Fundraising	4.25	1.17	.164	-.277*
Total Quality Management	4.20	.82	-.144	.320*
Public speaking	4.14	.84	-.048	-.165
Needs assessment	4.14	.84	.092	-.131
Managing a diverse workforce	4.12	1.01	-.160	.071
Personal growth and stress management	4.12	1.02	.076	-.043
Volunteer management	4.12	1.11	.290*	-.377**
Marketing	4.08	.90	.143	-.049
Staff compensation and evaluation	4.08	1.00	-.176	.015
Board recruitment and development	4.02	1.58	.199	-.340*
Grant writing	4.00	1.17	-.022	-.303*
Organizational mission development	3.98	1.13	.076	-.266

Table 6.1 (cont'd.)

Computers and software	3.89	.86	-.234	.202
Cost-benefit analysis	3.85	1.07	-.062	.059
Legal issues for nonprofits	3.83	1.02	-.272*	.357**
Board self-evaluation	3.55	1.17	-.063	-.262
Accounting	3.43	1.12	-.192	.070
Policy advocacy and lobbying	3.40	1.18	-.290*	-.043
History of philanthropy and nonprofits	2.52	1.11	-.011	-.100

*($p \leq .05$), ** ($p \leq .01$). Importance scale ranges from 1 = not at all important to 5 = very important.
[1] Chi-square analyses using a truncated scale for importance show same levels of significance.

raising, grant writing, volunteer management, and board recruitment and development as less important. Managers of larger staffs may be able to make greater use of principles of TQM than managers of smaller staffs, who are likely to have fewer resources to devote to a TQM program. Managers of larger staffs also may face more legal issues related to personnel than their colleagues with smaller staffs. The managers of larger staffs may have hired individuals specifically to carry out fund development and volunteer coordination, making it less critical for the managers personally to have skills and knowledge in these areas. Larger staffs also may compensate for weak or inactive boards. Organizations with smaller staffs may have to rely more heavily on the board and thus have managers who rate the area of board recruitment and development higher in importance.

Faculty and Students' Views of the Importance of the Areas. Table 6.2 presents the average ratings for managers, students, and faculty. The ratings that significantly differ ($p \leq .05$) are underlined. (For each area, a one-way analysis of variance was performed to identify significant differences in means. This was followed by a Scheffe test to identify which groups significantly differed. These tests are not reported in the chapter but are available from the author.) Even though a mean rating

Table 6.2
Mean Ratings and Rankings of Areas by Managers, Students, and Faculty

Skill and Knowledge Areas	Managers (N = 53)		Students (N = 54)		Faculty (N = 24)	
	Mean	Rank	Mean	Rank	Mean	Rank
Leadership	4.85	1	4.41	6	4.22	11
Ethics and values in nonprofits	4.79	2	4.19	13	4.40	4
Long-term planning	4.64	3	4.54	2	4.50	2
Financial management	4.58	4	4.28	9	4.39	5

Table 6.2 (cont'd.)

Conducting effective meetings	4.57	5	4.06	16	3.81	21
Creativity	4.54	6	4.76	1	4.10	13
Public relations	4.54	6	4.44	5	4.25	9
Interpersonal skills	4.50	8	4.48	3	4.24	10
Short-term planning	4.46	9	4.31	8	4.28	7
Managing change	4.42	10	4.20	12	3.82	20
Conflict management	4.28	11	3.79	23	3.61	24
Program evaluation	4.25	12	4.09	15	4.28	7
Collaboration and networking	4.25	12	4.45	4	4.06	14
Fundraising	4.25	12	4.26	10	4.56	1
Total Quality Management	4.20	15	3.41	30	3.25	30
Public speaking	4.14	16	4.39	7	3.94	17
Needs assessment	4.14	16	3.89	20	3.94	17
Managing a diverse workforce	4.12	18	3.78	24	3.63	22
Personal growth and stress management	4.12	18	3.93	19	3.63	22
Volunteer management	4.12	18	4.06	16	3.90	19
Marketing	4.08	21	3.89	20	4.00	15
Staff compensation and evaluation	4.08	21	3.68	27	3.56	25
Board recruitment and development	4.02	23	3.48	28	4.12	12
Grant writing	4.00	24	4.19	13	4.29	6
Organizational mission development	3.98	25	4.04	18	4.50	2
Computers and software	3.89	26	4.26	10	3.47	27
Cost-benefit analysis	3.85	27	3.69	26	3.47	27
Legal issues for nonprofits	3.83	28	3.87	22	4.00	15
Board self-evaluation	3.55	29	3.10	31	3.47	27
Accounting	3.43	30	3.44	29	3.19	31
Policy advocacy and lobbying	3.40	31	3.70	25	3.50	26
History of philanthropy and nonprofits	2.52	32	2.96	32	3.12	32

Underlined ratings significantly differ at the $(p \leq .05)$ level.

might be different among the groups, the relative ranking of the area might place it in the same grouping of importance. For example, managers and students place leadership within the top six areas, but their mean ratings are significantly different. Table 6.2 includes the relative rank of each area for each stakeholder group.

Students and faculty rate leadership, conducting effective meetings, conflict management, and TQM significantly lower than managers. Faculty members also rate managing change significantly lower. Students rate ethics and values in nonprofits and staff compensation and evaluation significantly lower. The only area students rate significantly higher than managers is computers and software, but the difference is significant at only the .07 level. The areas of difference highlight the unique perspectives of the different stakeholder groups and their potential contributions to discussions of curriculum design. Faculty members can offer a perspective informed by current research and thinking and tied to educational principles and philosophy. Managers can offer a strong grounding in the field, surfacing the realities of the workplace. Students may provide the service of keeping a focus on what the future workplace might be like. Possible explanations for the differences in ratings help to support these assumed stakeholder strengths.

The somewhat lower ranking of leadership by faculty may be due to the vagueness of the leadership concept. Leadership research has recently experienced a resurgence in interest after a period of competing definitions, unclear management implications, and lost faith (Den Hartog, Van Muijen, and Koopman, 1997; Fiedler, 1996). Some management textbooks do not even mention leadership (for example, Whetten and Cameron, 1991). Faculty members may be more cynical than managers about the possibility of developing someone's leadership skills. However, despite differences in the mean ratings of leadership, the relative rankings of the area indicate that all stakeholder groups are likely to agree that it should be covered as a core curriculum topic.

Conducting effective meetings is in the middle or bottom of the rankings by students and faculty. Faculty members and students are unlikely to support the managers' view that it is a very important area. Managers, who routinely find themselves in meetings, recognize the benefit of a meeting that is well run. Students, who are likely to be the stakeholder group with the least work experience, may not understand how frequently managers attend meetings (Whetten and Cameron, 1991). Faculty members may see the area as a practical skill without a strong theoretical base. However, there is growing emphasis in this society on teams, and new models for management education endorse training in teamwork (NASPAA, 1992). Understanding and managing the dynamics of meetings fit under the teamwork umbrella and in time may gain greater legitimacy as an academic subject.

Total Quality Management and conflict management have the greatest divergence in manager and faculty ratings. Faculty members may have more exposure to the current research on TQM that notes its limitations and predicts growing disinterest by the business sector (Hackman and Wageman, 1995; Gummer, 1996). Nonprofit managers may be less familiar with the specifics of TQM but, given its visibility, assume it is a valuable management tool for any nonprofit manager. Feedback from faculty suggests that TQM's value may be overrated by the managers.

All managers perform conflict management in their organizations. Unlike TQM, managers do not have to be trained in it to do it. The relevance that managers see in conflict management may be related more to their personal experiences than to exposure to the area from professional contacts or media. Faculty and student relative disinterest in the area may be due more to a lack of awareness of the prevalence of organizational conflicts and consequences than to any discouraging research findings or trends. Here we see the value of having feedback from managers to help ensure that curriculum addresses workplace needs.

The students rated ethics and values significantly lower than did managers, but the topic still places thirteenth in the students' order of importance. Students are unlikely to resist the incorporation of ethics instruction into their programs. Business and public administration schools are increasingly addressing ethics in courses (Menzel, 1997). The nonprofit managers' mean rating reinforces the value of this trend.

Although students may not have the practical grounding of the practicing managers nor the research background of the faculty, they may be good at envisioning what future workplaces will be like. The students' rating of computers and software is significantly higher than the managers' rating at the .07 level and the faculty's rating at the .006 level. Managers may have rated the importance of computers and software based on how they are currently using computer technology, not on how they expect to use it in the future. Students may have been more future-oriented in their responses. Given that computer systems will become increasingly important in the nonprofit sector (Moore, 1995; Greene, 1993), the students' mean rating of computers and software provides the best curriculum guide.

The managers, faculty, and students were given the opportunity to note additional skill and knowledge areas that they thought would be valuable to any nonprofit manager. Only one manager added an area: grassroots organizational skills. Faculty added entrepreneurial activity, organization design, writing skills, philosophy of voluntarism, and policy analysis. Students added the role of nonprofits in society, public/private partnerships, international NGOs, personal ethics, audience development/visitor behavior, crisis management, donor compliance, staff supervision, and consulting. Further consideration of these and other areas can lead to additional ideas for courses and course topics.

Connection of Findings to Other Work. Some of the skill and knowledge areas examined in this study have been discussed by others in attempts to develop curriculum guidelines. Van Til and Hegyesi (1996) asked members of the ISTR (International Society for Third Sector Research) Affinity Group on Education and Training to comment on the importance of some "classic management" and "basic sector-specific" courses. The ISTR group gave their highest endorsement to classic courses on program evaluation, human resource management, and leadership skills development. In this study, the corresponding skill and knowledge areas are all considered to be important, if not *very* important. The ISTR group gave a weaker endorsement to courses in planning and policy formulation and development. In this study, long-term planning is rated as a very important skill and short-term planning an important skill. Policy advocacy and lobbying is ranked among the less important areas. The ISTR group strongly supported sector-specific course work in ethics, marketing, and financial management. In this study these areas also are found to be very important or important. The ISTR group gave less support to history and literature of the sector, a result similar to that for history of philanthropy and nonprofits in this study.

The areas examined in this study include many of the "core competencies" for

Figure 6.1
Skill and Knowledge Areas for Any Nonprofit Manager

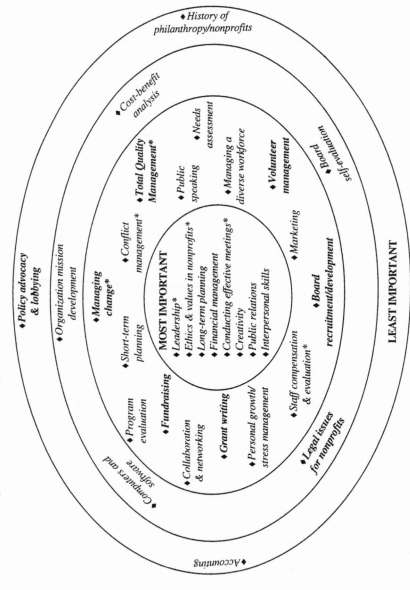

◆ History of philanthropy/nonprofits

◆ Cost-benefit analysis

◆ Needs assessment

◆ Policy advocacy & lobbying

◆ Organization mission development

Total Quality Management*

◆ Managing change*

◆ Conflict management*

◆ Public speaking

◆ Managing a diverse workforce

Volunteer management

◆ Short-term planning

MOST IMPORTANT

◆ Leadership*
◆ Ethics & values in nonprofits*
◆ Long-term planning
◆ Financial management
◆ Conducting effective meetings*
◆ Creativity
◆ Public relations
◆ Interpersonal skills

Board self-evaluation

◆ Program evaluation

◆ Marketing

Fundraising

◆ Grant writing

Board recruitment/development

◆ Collaboration & networking

◆ Personal growth/ stress management

◆ Staff compensation & evaluation*

Legal issues for nonprofits

■ Computers and software

■ Accounting

LEAST IMPORTANT

Areas in bold vary in importance depending on the staffing characteristics of the organization. Areas with asterisks have importance ratings by faculty or students significantly different from those of managers ($p \leq .05$).

nonprofit managers developed at the Clarion Conference by academics and practitioners (Rubin, Adamski, and Block, 1989). The conference participants noted the importance of attention to the mission, understanding the nonprofit sector's history and laws, having creativity, boundary spanning, motivational leadership, marketing, policy analysis, lobbying and advocacy, board and volunteer development and management, planning, accounting, program evaluation, public relations, meeting management, verbal and written communication, coalition building and collaboration, conflict management, and financial development. The participants did not prioritize these competencies. We see from the present study that most of the competency areas vary in their importance as perceived by managers, faculty, and students.

Recommendations. Assuming that the managers, faculty, and students generally have an accurate understanding of the skills and knowledge needed to be successful as a nonprofit manager, the ratings offer initial guidelines for curriculum development. Figure 6.1 presents a graphic representation of the prioritization of areas based on the managers' mean ratings. Any area that has a mean rating by faculty or students that is significantly lower ($p \leq .05$) than the managers' mean rating is indicated with an asterisk.

Programs that develop the skill and knowledge areas in the core and innermost ring are likely to be better at preparing students for nonprofit management careers than those that do not. Current practice might reflect this guideline. Wish and Mirabella's survey of colleges and universities found that most nonprofit management programs with three or more courses include a financial management course, a subject we found to be very important, and a generic nonprofit management course (which might cover any of the areas in our figure).

The subjects found in the center of the figure are stable regardless of workplace staffing. Some of the other subjects, indicated in bold, vary in importance depending on staffing characteristics. Students using the figure as a tool for course selection may wish to upgrade or downgrade the importance of the bolded areas to reflect the needs of their intended workplace. For example, students who plan to manage a volunteer-based organization should upgrade the importance of volunteer management. Students intending to work in organizations with larger professional staffs should consider training in legal issues for nonprofits.

The figure serves as a useful starting point or preliminary model for discussion of course offerings and content. Educational objectives, theoretical base for the areas, teaching philosophy, and available resources need to be considered to refine the prioritization of areas. Higher education programs should capture the unique strengths of their settings with a strong orientation to existing knowledge bases and pedagogy.

Perceived Benefit from Studying the Areas

The priorities for course topics presented in Figure 6.1 assume that students entering nonprofit management education programs are not already adequately prepared in the "very important" and "important" areas. In addition, it assumes that there is sufficient market demand for the areas to maintain course investments. To begin to see if these assumptions are met, we examined the benefit that practicing nonprofit managers believe they would get from studying the areas. We also examined the managers' interest in taking workshops or courses covering the areas. Students in nonprofit management programs may have varying levels of work experience. The managers in the sample help us see how students who have nonprofit management experience and who hold a full- or part-time job might respond to course topics.

Table 6.3 presents the managers' rating of the personal benefit they expect they could get from training in each area and their interest in attending a workshop or course covering each area. The areas are listed in order of mean benefit rating. On average, managers find that none of the areas is "very beneficial" to study. Of the eight core areas shown in Figure 6.1, only leadership, long-term planning, and public relations earn a mean rating of better than 3.8 on a five-point scale. The areas falling beneath the midpoint of the scale are history of philanthropy and nonprofits, policy advocacy and lobbying, and accounting. These are the same areas that earn the lowest mean ratings of importance.

Table 6.3
Managers' Perceived Benefit from Study of Areas and Percentage of Managers
Interested in Courses and Workshops Covering Areas

Skill and Knowledge Areas	Benefit to Respondent of Training in the Area		Interest in Course	Interest in Workshop
	Mean	Std. Dev.	Percent	Percent
Leadership	3.92	1.26	3.8	50.9
Long-term planning	3.88	1.32	13.2	49.1
Public relations	3.84	1.14	15.1	54.7
Fundraising	3.75	1.45	17.0	54.7
Total Quality Management	3.75	1.09	9.4	49.1
Managing change	3.70	1.27	9.4	43.4
Conflict management	3.66	1.27	15.1	47.2
Computers and software	3.66	1.44	13.2	41.5
Creativity	3.63	1.37	7.5	37.7
Personal growth and stress management	3.62	1.34	9.4	47.2
Grant writing	3.59	1.45	11.3	50.9
Program evaluation	3.53	1.24	11.3	39.6
Conducting effective meetings	3.50	1.23	3.8	52.8
Financial management	3.49	1.48	17.0	35.8
Board recruitment and development	3.46	1.45	5.7	58.5
Interpersonal skills	3.45	1.26	3.8	37.7
Ethics and values in nonprofits	3.44	1.25	3.8	37.5
Needs assessment	3.43	1.24	7.5	45.3

Table 6.3 (cont'd.)

Volunteer				
management	3.42	1.30	13.2	49.1
Marketing	3.41	1.27	11.3	50.9
Managing a diverse				
workforce	3.41	1.21	5.7	45.3
Cost-benefit analysis	3.39	1.32	9.4	37.7
Short-term planning	3.37	1.33	7.5	43.4
Collaboration and				
networking	3.34	1.29	3.8	34.0
Staff compensation				
and evaluation	3.34	1.29	11.3	41.5
Public speaking	3.18	1.40	7.5	37.7
Organizational				
mission				
development	3.14	1.34	5.7	39.6
Board self-evaluation	3.12	1.41	3.8	45.3
Legal issues for				
nonprofits	3.08	1.23	9.4	35.8
Policy advocacy and				
lobbying	2.88	1.39	3.8	37.7
Accounting	2.54	1.31	11.3	24.5
History of				
philanthropy and				
nonprofits	2.25	1.30	11.3	20.8

Scale for benefit from studying area ranges from 1 = not at all beneficial to 5 = very beneficial.

The larger standard deviations for benefit versus importance show that there is greater disagreement among respondents on which areas are personally beneficial to study than on their importance to any nonprofit manager. This suggests that personal and organizational characteristics of respondents influence ratings of personal benefit.

Table 6.4 presents correlations of expected personal benefit with personal and organizational characteristics. The table shows that having an undergraduate degree has little influence on the perceived benefit of studying most of the areas. Managers with degrees rate board recruitment and development significantly higher than managers without degrees. Managers without degrees rate the benefit of studying legal issues for nonprofits significantly higher. Work experience in the nonprofit sector and affiliation with an association make more difference than education. Less experienced managers are a more eager market for study than their more senior colleagues. Amount of experience is negatively and significantly related to 25 percent of the areas. Managers of organizations affiliated with an association see significantly more benefit than unaffiliated managers in studying 44 percent of the areas. Perhaps exposure to training materials and activities through an association makes managers more aware of the benefit of continued education.

Staffing characteristics are related to benefit ratings for only a few of the areas.

Managers in volunteer-based organizations indicate more benefit from studying board recruitment and development than managers who rely less on volunteers. Managers of volunteer-based organizations see less benefit from studying interpersonal skills, despite the special motivational challenges inherent in working with volunteers (Pearce, 1993; Ilsley, 1990). They also see less benefit from studying cost-benefit analysis and program evaluation, techniques useful for judging the effectiveness of programs. The more informal nature of many of the volunteer-based programs may make these techniques seemingly unnecessary for continued survival and legitimacy. Managers with smaller professional staffs expect to gain more from studying fundraising and board recruitment and development. Managers with fewer professional staff members may not have employees focusing on fundraising and may have greater need for more active and committed boards. Other personal and organizational characteristics may have influenced the benefit ratings but could not be examined in this study.

Table 6.4
Correlations of Expected Benefit from Studying Areas with Personal and Organizational Characteristics of Managers

Skill and Knowledge Areas	Undergraduate Degree[1]	Years of Nonprofit Experience	Volunteer-Based Organization[1]	Number of Professional Paid Staff	Part of an Association
Leadership	.274	-.161	.038	-.010	.292*
Long-term planning	.287*	-.216	.052	.031	.150
Public relations	.174	-.523**	-.045	-.167	.331*
Fundraising	.374**	-.244	.199	-.379**	.259
Total Quality Management	.000	.074	-.095	.246	.173
Managing change	.340*	.070	-.090	.136	.221
Conflict management	-.037	-.232	.219	.007	.023
Computers and software	.306*	-.170	-.228	.140	.446**
Creativity	.311*	-.004	-.103	.161	.290*
Personal growth and stress management	-.022	-.102	.103	.034	.421**
Grant writing	.305*	-.452**	.043	-.232	.041
Program evaluation	.374**	-.259	-.288*	.104	.321*
Conducting effective meetings	.205	-.093	-.110	.110	.393**
Financial management	.093	-.359**	-.081	.000	.267
Board recruitment and development	.337*	-.160	.370**	-.374**	.135
Interpersonal skills	.247	-.100	-.284*	.195	.443**
Ethics and values in nonprofits	.303*	-.072	-.077	.093	.390**

Table 6.4 (cont'd.)

Needs assessment	.339*	-.269	-.213	.070	.356*
Volunteer management	-.068	-.388**	.196	-.161	.411**
Marketing	.102	-.361**	-.043	-.072	.156
Managing a diverse workforce	-.012	-.010	-.134	.144	.192
Cost-benefit analysis	.395**	-.244	-.317*	.126	.350*
Short-term planning	.172	-.198	-.075	.141	.084
Collaboration and net working	.376**	-.219	.091	-.162	.243
Staff compensation & evaluation	.275	-.155	-.069	.132	.266
Public speaking	.070	-.399**	-.185	-.039	.111
Organization mission development	.317*	-.385**	-.039	-.001	.314*
Board self-evaluation	.290*	-.215	.183	-.263	-.050
Legal issues for nonprofits	.288*	-.035	-.130	.131	.302*
Policy advocacy and lobbying	.325*	-.016	-.151	.004	.236
Accounting	-.010	-.386**	-.135	.040	.267
History of philanthropy and nonprofits	.026	-.218	-.133	.020	.244

$(N = 53)$, * $(p \leq .05)$, ** $(p \leq .01)$.

[1] Chi-square analyses using a truncated scale for the importance of the areas show the same significant relationships. Measures: Scale for benefit from studying areas ranges from 1 = not at all beneficial to 5 = very beneficial. Dichotomous measures are "manager has undergraduate degree," "volunteer-based organization," and "organization is part of an association." Continuous variables are "years of experience in the nonprofit sector" and "number of professional paid staff members."

Recommendations. The data on expected benefits suggest that in-service students (students currently working in nonprofit management positions) may have different needs than pre-service students (students who have not yet started their management careers). For example, students who have never coordinated activities and set work goals may see more benefit in studying short-term planning than managers who do this routinely. Program designers should identify the type(s) of students they wish to reach. Programs provided for students with substantial to no work experience need to be more flexible than programs for a more narrow population.

Nonprofit education providers should recognize that many nonprofit managers do not have undergraduate degrees (37 percent in this sample). Programs that offer only graduate-level courses exclude managers without degrees who can benefit from the expertise of faculty and interactive learning in a classroom setting. Yet a typical undergraduate class at many universities and colleges is composed of students in their early twenties with little or no work experience in nonprofits. Practicing nonprofit managers wandering into such a class may be far above their classmates in their understanding of management. Faculty members teaching an undergraduate nonprofit management course need to be familiar with their students' backgrounds, acknowledging knowledge and skills developed "in the field" and offering appropriate learning challenges.

Characteristics of a manager's organization may influence his or her perceptions of the benefit that can be derived from studying an area. Nonprofit management education programs that fail to recognize the diversity of the sector may miss opportunities to target some of their offerings to the types of nonprofit managers that believe they can gain the most benefit from them. Research can help to sort students and organizations according to specific management education needs. Targeted marketing plans can then be devised to provide managers with information about relevant courses.

Managers' Interest and Use of Educational Options

Managers have a variety of options for developing skills and knowledge helpful for managing nonprofits. The last two columns of Table 6.3 show the managers' interest in pursuing workshops and college courses in the 32 areas examined in the study. Interest in taking a workshop or course is not solely dependent on expected benefit. For example, training in leadership has the highest mean rating of personal benefit, but a course covering the area interests only 4 percent of the managers. History of philanthropy and nonprofits, in contrast, has the lowest rating of personal benefit but a course covering the area interests 11 percent of the managers. Managers may appreciate the opportunity to take courses that they do not initially believe have direct benefits.

Managers are more interested in workshops than courses. More than 50 percent of the respondents are interested in workshops on leadership, conducting effective meetings, public relations, fundraising, marketing, board recruitment and development, and grant writing. The areas with the most interest as courses are financial management, fundraising, public relations, conflict management, long-term planning, volunteer management, and computers and software. These course topics are attractive to 13 percent to 17 percent of the respondents. Shorter workshops and courses generally attract more interest than longer ones. Table 6.5 shows the self-reported likelihood of using different educational formats. The format most likely to be used is a one-day workshop or seminar.

The managers' preferences may be explained partially by the barriers they perceive in pursuing education. Table 6.6 shows that cost and time away from work are the biggest barriers. About 59 percent of the managers' organizations provide funding for training of paid staff, and 16 percent provide training funds for volunteers and board members. Financial support is usually limited to coverage of workshop and conference expenses.

Table 6.7 reports the percentage of managers using courses as well as other education sources. Many nonprofit managers in Bloomington are taking advantage of courses despite the required financial and time investment. However, consistent with data presented in earlier tables, they are making more use of conferences and workshops.

Table 6.5
Self-Reported Likelihood of Managers Using Different Formats for Education

Educational Formats	Likelihood of Using Format	
	Mean	Std. Dev.
Set of courses for college degree	1.88	1.27
Semester-long course	2.20	1.50
3 week college course	2.80	1.34
6 week college course	2.68	1.33
3 day workshop	3.77	1.18
1 day workshop or seminar	4.43	.96
1-2 hour workshop or seminar	4.39	1.15

($N = 53$). Scale ranges from 1 = not at all likely to 5 = very likely.

Table 6.6
Significance of Different Barriers in Pursuing Education in Nonprofit Management

Barriers	Significance of Barrier	
	Mean	Std. Dev.
Cost of training	4.42	.98
Time away from work while training	4.21	1.07
Local availability of training	3.90	1.01
Lack of staff interest in getting training	2.10	1.25
Lack of board interest in getting training	2.38	1.35

($N = 53$). Scale ranges from 1 = not at all significant to 5 = very significant.

Table 6.7
Percentage of Nonprofit Managers Using Education Sources

Source	Use of Local Source (within 60 miles of office)	Use of Non-Local source	Use of Either
Professional conferences	72	75	94
Training workshops	74	51	83
Professional trade publications	not applicable	not applicable	68
Books	not applicable	not applicable	66
Training by other nonprofits	45	15	55
College/university courses	41	9	45
Executive speaker seminars	34	19	40
Independent consultants	32	15	38
Fund Raising School courses	21	19	30

($N = 53$).

Recommendations. Students who have full- or part-time jobs may have cost and time constraints that encourage them to look outside a university setting for nonprofit management education. Scholarships for in-service students can help overcome cost barriers. Courses or course modules that maintain pedagogical integrity without using traditional semester or term-long formats may help address the problem of time away from work.

Higher education is one node in a network of nonprofit education providers. Students should be encouraged to consider multiple sources for education. Workshops, conferences, seminars, and speaker series cannot replace courses but can serve as a supplement and help fill market demands. Programs based in universities and colleges are limited in what they can and should cover. Outside training sources tend to offer more personal stories and "rules of thumb" than principles and analysis based on theory and research, but they still offer considerable benefits. For example, students participating in outside training can gain perspectives from the field, learn professional norms and trends, discover emerging knowledge and technology, and develop professional contacts.

What Managers Desire in Applicants for Nonprofit Management Positions

Nonprofit programs can better prepare future nonprofit leaders for their job searches and duties by learning what practicing managers are looking for in new hires. Managers in the study were asked to rate the importance of different educational and work experiences to an applicant seeking a position similar to their own position. Table 6.8 provides a summary of the managers' ratings of the importance of potential hiring criteria. The managers place most hiring emphasis on the applicants' work experience in a similar organization. Volunteer work experience in an organization similar to their own has the second greatest importance to hiring decisions but is still close to the midpoint of the importance scale.

Table 6.8
Importance of Different Educational and Work Experiences to an Applicant
for a Position Similar to the Respondent's Position

Applicant Experiences	Importance to Hiring Decision	
	Mean	Std. Dev.
Previous work in similar organization	4.27	.88
Previous volunteering in similar organization	3.31	1.27
Any type of work experience	3.15	1.46
Participation in nonprofit management workshops	3.10	1.16
Any type of volunteer experience	3.02	1.31
Any type of college degree	2.98	1.54
Courses in nonprofit management	2.75	1.17
A college program in nonprofit management	2.61	1.22

($N = 53$). Scale ranges from 1 = not at all important to 5 = very important.

The managers in the study are not particularly impressed by applicants with non-profit management degrees or courses in nonprofit management. Both earn an average rating below the midpoint on a five-point importance scale. Haas and Robinson (1996), on the other hand, found that a graduate degree in nonprofit management was valuable for candidates for middle or upper nonprofit management positions. (Managers in the Haas and Robinson study had no degree preferences, rating a master's in nonprofit management, MBA, and MA in a relevant field around a 2 on a four-point scale, with 1 indicating "very valuable" and 4 indicating "not at all valuable.") The managers in this study were not asked to rate the value of educational and work credentials. Instead, they rated how important these credentials are to hiring decisions. According to the managers, courses or a program in nonprofit management are not required for applicants for nonprofit management positions and make relatively little difference to a hiring decision compared to the applicants' work and volunteer experiences.

Personal and organizational characteristics of the managers have little relationship to their ratings of the hiring criteria. Correlation of years of work experience and number of professional staff with the ratings revealed no significant relationships. Belief in the importance of having any type of college degree is significantly and positively related to whether or not the manager has an undergraduate degree (.560, $p < .001$). Also, managers from volunteer-based organizations see more value than their colleagues in applicants' work and volunteer experience (.362, $p = .01$, for any type of work experience and .339, $p = .02$, for any type of volunteer experience).

Recommendations. Experiential learning is increasingly being promoted by educators in the management field (e.g., Dinmore, 1997; Olshfski, 1994; Bruce, 1993). The managers' ratings of potential hiring criteria further emphasize the importance of activities outside the classroom to help prepare students for job searches and careers. Students' participation in internships, service-learning activities, independent volunteering, conferences, and workshops should be encouraged. These activities are likely to make graduates more attractive to potential employers. They also are opportunities for further development of students' knowledge and skills. An added benefit is that managers' exposure to well-trained students may increase the managers' evaluation of the general value of higher education and the specific value of nonprofit management education.

Outreach to nonprofit managers to inform them of the value of education in nonprofit management may be useful in some communities. However, greater awareness of and interest in nonprofit management education may occur as more professionally prepared graduates enter or return to the nonprofit sector's labor force. Students graduating from nonprofit management programs who display needed skills and knowledge in their jobs will help to legitimate their programs and add credibility to future job applicants with similar educational backgrounds.

DISCUSSION

This chapter offers a case study of how three types of stakeholders in one community view aspects of nonprofit management education. The sample sizes for the analyses are small, and the specific findings need to be corroborated by other studies to show the extent of their generalizability. Nonprofit management education providers in other communities may find different priorities of the skill and knowledge areas, perceived benefit from study of the areas, use of education sources, and hiring criteria. The views of nonprofit managers, faculty members, and students on important areas for study are likely to be largely similar, but any differences may be enlightening and lead to program improvements. By researching variations in communities and differences among stakeholders' views, nonprofit management education providers can get a better sense of how they can best serve their students and the nonprofit sector.

The study has five broad implications: (1) Nonprofit management programs cannot develop all the skills and knowledge areas useful to nonprofit managers. Prioritization of these areas is necessary and possible. (2) Not all nonprofit management students have the same needs and interests. Understanding the student population for a program can help in making decisions about program flexibility, course offerings and content, and marketing strategies. (3) Reducing financial costs and time away from work may make courses more feasible for some nonprofit managers. Scholarships and shorter course formats may help attract in-service students. (4) College and university programs are part of a larger network of formal and informal education providers. Students should be encouraged to take advantage of learning opportunities outside the classroom. For example, support systems can be established to help students engage in volunteer work, attend conferences, and participate in workshops. (5) Nonprofit management course work has little weight in some hiring circles. Job-seekers may need to make potential employers aware of the content and value of their program. However, if students are educated well, the reputation of nonprofit management education programs and their graduates can grow.

7

Nonprofit Undergraduate Education: Delivery Models for Curricula within the American Humanics Program

Norman A. Dolch, Roland Kidwell, Jr., Jeffrey Sadow, and Jimmie Smith

The American Humanics Program (AHP) is currently the only nationally recognized undergraduate program specifically training human service professionals for nonprofit organizations. Unlike graduate programs designed for working adults looking to make a career change or nonprofit professionals seeking credentialing for promotion, AHP certification seeks to instill in undergraduates a sense of mission toward nonprofits and prepare them for entry-level jobs. Undergraduates often want to work with people in human service organizations, but they fear a lack of job opportunities or low pay. American Humanics, with its national/nonprofit partners, has identified the competencies that make undergraduates most desirable to nonprofits, equal to employees who have been on the job for one year.

Undergraduate nonprofit management education has received little attention. The 1986 conference on nonprofit management education gave only passing attention to the undergraduate level (O'Neill and Young, 1988, pp. 19, 98), and a recent survey of programs did not include undergraduate work (see Chapter 2 of this book). Yet nonprofits have traditionally hired baccalaureate degree holders. Just having a degree was often enough, and training occurred on the job. Just as the private sector has changed greatly over the last 25 years, so has the nonprofit sector. With devolution and greater emphasis on efficiency and effectiveness, nonprofits are increasingly looking for entry-level professionals who already have training. American Humanics has been doing this type of training since 1948.

American Humanics was founded by Roe Bartle, affectionately known as the "Chief" in his beloved Kansas City, Missouri. The nickname "Chief" referred to his long-time work in Boy Scouts and other community philanthropic activities. The goal of Bartle's Humanics Program, a term which he coined, was originally to train college men to become Boy Scout executives. The first AHP program was located at Missouri Valley College, which even today has one of the largest and most successful programs in terms of student participation.

AHP expanded to train students, both men and women, for other major youth organizations and today has a partnership with Big Brothers/Big Sisters of America; Boys and Girls Clubs of America; Boy Scouts of America; Camp Fire Boys and Girls; Girls, Inc.; Girl Scouts of the USA; Junior Achievement, Inc.; National Network for Youth; YMCA of the USA; and YWCA of the USA. In the 1960s, AHP went beyond training professionals for youth work to training professionals for nonprofit human service entry-level leadership positions. This development took place as AHP became sponsored on the national level by the American Red Cross and later by Habitat for Humanity, United Way of America, and Volunteers of America.

The program is offered on 40 campuses throughout the United States. Each year, 100 students complete the requirements for AHP certification, and an additional 200 students graduate from the various programs with either classroom or other formal training in nonprofit management. There was a demand from the 15 national partners of AHP for over 10,000 entry-level managers in 1997. These affiliates support American Humanics because they view graduates as having skills and knowledge equivalent to employees with one year of job experience. The skills and knowledge emanate from the competencies that make up the AHP certificate. Competencies cluster around the four broad knowledge areas of nonprofit organizational theory and research, nonprofit accounting, volunteerism, and fundraising.

Besides emphasizing competencies, the AHP strives to identify students who have a mission orientation, meaning a personal understanding and affirmation of the importance of nonprofit work as well as a passion for that work. This mission orientation is central to the AHP and complements the skills and techniques taught in the program. Through co-curricular activities such as participation in the campus student organization and internships, AHP often screens out students who do not have passion for nonprofit work.

Considerable flexibility is found when comparing curricula on AHP campuses. Four models have been identified: (1) certificate programs, (2) academic minors, (3) academic majors, and (4) combinations of academic majors and minors. In each model, students who complete the requirements receive an AHP certificate. Each of these models is examined below and compared relative to funding, governance, and interdisciplinary cooperation. Comparisons are based on interviews with the campus directors of the various programs and results of a student survey on the four representative campuses. On the basis of the interviews and student survey results, advantages and disadvantages of the four models are discussed. Trends in undergraduate higher education regarding experiential education are also examined.

FOUR AMERICAN HUMANICS DELIVERY MODELS

The four delivery models for the AHP curriculum are a certificate program at Louisiana State University in Shreveport; an academic minor in youth agency administration at Murray State University in Kentucky; an academic major, the Bachelor of Science degree in Recreation Administration, at Arizona State University; and a combined academic major and minor, the Human Service Agency Management degree at Lindenwood College in Missouri. These are compared on the basis of in-depth telephone interviews with the campus directors of the programs and written materials on the programs.

Certificate Program at Louisiana State University in Shreveport

Louisiana State University in Shreveport (LSUS) offers the AHP as a certificate that any student may earn while working on the requirements for his/her major. Some students who hold degrees have also enrolled to receive the certificate. Required courses for certification total 22 hours. Students are required to take accounting (three hours), organization theory and research (three hours), marketing (three hours), practicum in nonprofit organizations (one hour, but may be repeated for up to three hours credit), seminar in not-for-profit organizations (three hours), internship (six hours), and the American Humanics Training Institute (one hour). Many of the AHP courses are cross-listed in management, political science, psychology, and sociology. Most students seeking AHP certification are enrolled in these majors. Because the course work is part of their major, the LSUS American Humanics Program is very student-friendly. There is also an option in the General Studies Degree for a concentration in Applied Sciences, which may be met through AHP courses.

The LSUS program officially began in the fall of 1995. It is housed in the Department of History and Social Science within the College of Liberal Arts. Certificate programs at LSUS are under the auspices of the Dean of Continuing Education and Public Service. Students participating in the program are expected to maintain continuous enrollment in the noncredit course "American Humanics Leadership Development" and pay a $25 fee each semester for this noncredit course. This course provides a fall and spring retreat, a monthly seminar or workshop for the students, T-shirts, notebooks, and other benefits.

An important aspect of the program is the American Humanics Student Organization, which is officially recognized by the Student Organization Council on campus. This is the co-curricular aspect of the program that gives students opportunities to practice leadership, fundraising, and other competencies developed by the program. For example, the club sold telephone calling cards for Valentine's Day and marketed the cards' voice mail as a way to leave a personal Valentine message. Proceeds of the sale were used to support attendance in the American Humanics Training Institute, an annual event organized by American Humanics as a capstone learning experience. American Humanics at LSUS prepares students for entry-level positions with youth and human service nonprofits. This is the philosophy underlying every aspect of the program. Each required course deals with some of the competencies that students must master to receive certification. Besides participation in program activities, students are encouraged to do volunteer work in programs to gain additional experience.

Direction for the program is provided by Norman A. Dolch, who is a professor of sociology. He became acquainted with American Humanics through his work with the National Volunteer Staff of Camp Fire Boys and Girls. When LSUS was searching for ways to connect the campus with the community, Dolch suggested the program and also pointed out that it would provide a program especially for the training of service-sector workers, something which the campus lacked.

Because of a 30 percent budget reduction over the last five years, the university approved moving forward with the program only if outside funds could be found for its operation. An advisory committee of faculty and nonprofit representatives was formed. Funding is provided by nonprofits, which sign agreements for service at the $1,000, $500, or $250 level. By signing agreements and placing money on deposit with the university, the nonprofits receive places at workshops for their employees, preferential internship placement, and limited access to community needs assessments and customized program evaluation research. The advisory committee meets monthly to make decisions regarding the program.

Unlike several other universities or colleges, LSUS does not provide any direct funding for AHP. Nonprofit support seems strong; about 35 nonprofit executive directors and community professionals serve as unpaid adjunct faculty to the program. In 1996–97, there were 40 students officially in the program. At a commuter campus like LSUS, the $25 noncredit course fee commits the student to the program, and no student who is in the program seems to feel that it is unfair or burdensome. As of May 1997, seven students had completed the LSUS program. Students come primarily from the Shreveport–Bossier City area of Louisiana (about 300,000 in population). About 90 percent of LSUS students remain in this area.

Academic Minor at Murray State University

At Murray State University (MSU), AHP participants have the opportunity to obtain an academic minor in Youth Agency Administration. A core curriculum of 19 hours in youth agency administration is supplemented by six hours of restricted electives from specific courses such as psychology, recreation, and social work. The core curriculum consists of courses in current trends and issues in community service, introduction to youth agency administration, leadership and support systems for youth agency administration, fundraising, six hours of internship with an agency, and a senior seminar for one credit.

For electives, students choose two three-credit courses in areas as diverse as accounting, environmental education, outdoor recreation, ethics, and adolescent psychology. In deciding upon electives, students first discuss their interests and goals with the AHP director. Students interested in working with youth might take courses in adolescent psychology. Interpersonal communications is one of the more popular electives.

The MSU program, which began in 1983, is known as the American Humanics Center for Leadership in Community Service. The Murray State AHP philosophy is "to prepare students for leadership and volunteer roles in youth, human service and other nonprofit organizations." There are no specific philosophies for each course, although service learning takes place in all core courses. A key element of the program is the concept of service learning. Students learn constructs and theories within each AHP course and then supplement this learning with experience in providing community service. In the introductory course (Current Trends and Issues in Community Service), the large class size requires that the experiential activity be pursued on an individual basis. In the other courses, students take part in a collective class project.

There are 150 students taking AHP courses, and 85 to 90 percent of these are in the Youth Agency Administration minor. A few students who take AHP courses are not pursuing a minor, and several graduate students are taking the courses while pursuing a master's degree in human service. Roger Weis, the campus director of the program, teaches all of the AHP courses. Three courses are offered each regular semester. The fundraising course is offered during the summer semester. There is little interdisciplinary involvement in the MSU program, although speakers from other disciplines are sometimes invited to speak to AHP classes. For example, a communication professor might talk about conflict resolution with the leadership class.

A 15-member advisory committee consists of professors from organizational communication, recreation, and education; administrators and staff such as the Vice President for Student Affairs; and five representatives from local nonprofits. This advisory committee meets twice a year. Members of the advisory committee are nominated by the Dean of the College of Education. The advisory committee plays a supportive but not very active role in the program.

The AHP is part of the Health, Physical Education, and Recreation (HPER) Department. The program is governed as part of the HPER department but is given a great deal of autonomy. The Murray State AHP is a line item in the general university budget. Students do not pay extra fees to take AHP courses or to enroll in the minor. The only outside funding sought is for students to attend the annual American Humanics Training Institute, and this project is part of the fundraising course. Both the previous and current university administration are committed to the program and have provided a substantial budget.

There are about 30 graduates with the minor in Youth Agency Administration each year. Anecdotal evidence of the program's success comes from individual students. Students from the program are placed in agencies if they so desire. The program director says that all students who want to work in a nonprofit and who request help in locating a position get a job within three months of graduation. The required internship is helpful in eventually getting students permanent placement with nonprofit organizations—if not at the agency of internship, then a related one. About 85 percent of internships are paid positions. Serving an unpaid internship would put a financial hardship on most of the students because they must leave Murray, Kentucky, with its population of 20,000, and go somewhere such as Bowling Green, St. Louis, or Nashville for a summer internship of six credit hours. All but 5 percent of the student internships take place during the summer.

Academic Major at Arizona State University

Arizona State University (ASU) offers a Bachelor of Science degree in Recreation Administration with a specialty in Youth Agency Administration. To receive the American Humanics Certificate with their degree, students complete 26 hours of formal course work: fundraising (three hours), volunteerism (three hours), youth and human services workshop (four hours), American Humanics Institute (one hour), managing not-for-profit agencies (three hours), and a senior internship (12 hours). The primary target population for the program consists of undergraduates who desire a career of leadership in nonprofit youth and human service organizations. The mission of the Arizona State AHP is expressed in the very meaning of the word "humanics," according to campus director Robert Ashcraft, who says that it is to attract, prepare, and place students into leadership positions with our nation's most respected nonprofit youth and human service organizations.

Driving the certification is the achievement of competencies specified by American Humanics, Inc. The formal classroom experiences are only part of the training program. Co-curricular experiences are an extremely important aspect of the program and include having students volunteer to work with agencies and programs or participate in the campus student organization. The program emphasizes research, theory, philosophy, skills, and experiential learning in which students have an opportunity to apply their learning.

The AHP resides in the College of Public Programs and the Department of Recreation Management and Tourism. Although the program is governed by this college and department, a community board assists with community relations and fundraising. Half of the program's budget comes from the university budget and half from fundraising.

The major in Recreation Management is interdisciplinary by nature and requires American Humanics Students to be engaged across disciplines. Faculty interact with one another across disciplines primarily through collaborative research. Eight faculty are responsible for the program and all hold doctoral degrees. Adjunct faculty include the executive director of the Maricopa Volunteer Center, the president of the Phoenix Boys and Girls Clubs, and the executive director of the Camp Fire Council of Central Arizona.

The program at ASU has a 90 percent placement rate for students who wish to work after graduation rather than pursue other choices such as graduate education. While direct placement of graduates in a nonprofit organization is the goal of Arizona State University's AHP, students who pursue other careers are not considered failures. These former students usually assume such roles as volunteer board member and donor, which add great value to any community. These students may have been introduced to nonprofit involvement through AHP. The Arizona State AHP provides education on the role and scope of nonprofit organizations, which may result in student employment opportunities, enhanced participation in nonprofit organizations, and enhanced quality of life for individuals and communities.

Combination (Certificate, Academic Major and Minor) at Lindenwood College in Missouri

At Lindenwood College, a private college of about 6,000 students in St. Charles, Missouri, outside of St. Louis, students may choose to major in Human Service Agency Management (HSAM). Lindenwood advertises this as a baccalaureate degree for students who are interested in "careers in youth and human service agencies." Students must complete the 18-hour HSAM core curriculum: introduction to human service agencies (three hours), management of human service agencies (three hours), leadership (three hours), fundraising and financial management (three hours), internship (three hours), and senior synthesis (three hours). Other optional courses include the American Humanics Management Institute (one hour), special topics (one to three hours), and leisure studies (three hours).

To complete the major, each student must also earn 18 hours in one of the following four "areas of emphasis" for a total of 36 hours: management, recreation management, social science, and gerontology. For those who choose a traditional major in psychology, sociology, or business management, HSAM certification becomes an academic minor. Other students who have already earned a degree may complete the HSAM requirements as a "certificate program."

Because the HSAM degree cuts across so many academic areas, faculty across the campus have been very supportive of the program. Brian Watkins, the executive director of AHP, is the only faculty member teaching exclusively in the program. All other faculty come from existing departments. The entire program is funded as any other department would be in the general budget. Students use the fundraising course to raise 100 percent of the funds needed to attend the American Humanics Management Institute.

There are 44 students enrolled in the program, 23 women and 21 men. Most students are of traditional age, but many are older and "retraining," especially single mothers. Lindenwood has had no problems placing graduates who wish to begin their career in agencies in the metropolitan St. Louis area.

Similarities and Differences

There are several similarities and differences among the four models. For the most part, regardless of the curriculum model used, the campus cases appear very similar. The major difference appears in the case of the Murray State University program (academic minor), which is less interdisciplinary in emphasis than the others and in which all the courses are taught by one faculty member, who is the AHP program director. There are some differences in funding: The LSUS program is totally self-supporting, the Lindenwood College program is totally college-funded, and the other two are a combination of internal and external funds. Governance typically involves both internal (department, college) and community (local nonprofit agency) representatives. The programs with graduates have had a placement rate of 90 to 100 percent. All four programs focus on preparing undergraduates for leadership (staff and volunteer) roles in youth and human service agencies. All four are open to both current students and graduates. At Murray State, all courses are taught by the faculty member who is the AHP director; at the other three institutions, courses are taught by regular and adjunct faculty. The great number of similarities regardless of curriculum model is undoubtedly due to the influence of the American Humanics certification competencies and the philosophy that permeates the programs.

Student Survey Results

A survey of eight demographic and 31 opinion items was administered to students on the four campuses. Questionnaires were distributed to students on the campuses through various means such as classes. Completion of the questionnaires was voluntary. The number of responses and number of questionnaires distributed were as follows: certification program (LSUS: 19/40), academic minor (MSU: 39/150), academic major (ASU: 25/40), and the academic major-minor combination (Lindenwood College: 14/40). While not a random sample of students in the American Humanics Programs on these campuses, the responses can provide some insight on how students in different types of curriculum delivery models feel about the AHP.

The great majority (80+ percent) of the respondents were under 30 years of age, except for those in the LSUS certificate program, where 63 percent were over 30. Women constituted 95 percent of the respondents at LSUS, 49 percent at MSU, 64 percent at ASU, and 58 percent at Lindenwood. Whites made up 85+ percent of respondents at MSU, ASU, and Lindenwood and 52 percent at LSU.

The student opinion responses were formed into five indices on employment success, expectation, knowledge gained, positive aspects, and usefulness. The Cronbach's alpha for each index was greater than .70. A description of each index is found in Appendix 7.1. Table 7.1 reports the analysis of variance for student perceptions of selected program aspects. No difference is found between the programs on any of the indices. Although the results must be interpreted cautiously because of the nonrandom nature and small size of the sample, this finding reinforces the earlier observation about the similarities of the four models. Evidently, students are perceiving the American Humanics Program similarly regardless of the model of program delivery on their campus.

Table 7.1
Analysis of Variance for Student Perceptions on Selected Program Aspects between AHP Types

	Program types				
Student perceptions of AHP	Cert. $(N = 19)$	Minor $(N = 39)$	Major $(N = 25)$	Combination $(N = 14)$	P
Employment success	6.00	5.54	5.20	3.86	n.s.
Expectation index	10.21	10.77	10.36	8.29	n.s.
Knowledge gained index	15.12	15.33	14.82	13.69	n.s.
Positive aspects index	10.84	9.95	10.36	8.50	n.s.
Usefulness index	5.42	5.31	4.92	4.21	n.s.

Cert. = certification program (LSUS)
Minor = academic minor (MSU)
Major = academic major (ASU)
Combination = combination of an academic major and minor (Lindenwood)

Advantages and Disadvantages of the Curriculum Delivery Models

A 1985 report of the Association of American Colleges titled "Integrity in the College Curriculum" (Project, 1985) expressed the pessimistic view that majors and minors are not so much knowledge experiences as they are bureaucratic conveniences allowing professors to indulge their preoccupations and deans to control the flow of students around the campus. Discipline, according to the report, is any study that leads to knowledge; in this sense, it cannot be restricted to one academic department. History, for example, is everywhere in the curriculum. It is in the history of English literature, the art of the Renaissance, and the history of economic thought. Analogously, education in nonprofit leadership is found in the motivational theories of psychology, the small group dynamics of sociology, and the study of ethics in philosophy.

The four AHP curriculum models are interdisciplinary, except for the MSU minor program. All are competency-driven rather than discipline-driven. All AHP curricula delivery are results of faculty and deans making decisions for a variety of reasons to offer the certification. A distinct political advantage of the certification model is that it does not take majors away from anyone but rather enhances job opportunities of students regardless of major. All four models have the potential for attracting students. Certification programs, for example, can attract both traditional and non-traditional students as well as current degree holders already working in nonprofit organizations who wish to pursue the certification for credentialing purposes.

RELATIONSHIP OF DELIVERY MODELS TO SELECTED HIGHER EDUCATION TRENDS

Certification Programs

Universities are by definition institutions influenced by constituencies in the marketplace of society, which include professional groups (see Harridan, 1991, p. 453). Part of what they do for these professional groups such as teachers and human service workers is credentialing, a mechanism for setting standards of practice competency. These standards may be distinguished from professionalism, which encompasses behavior or attitude (Patterson and Vitello, 1994). Certification is a type of credentialing that verifies the ability to demonstrate adequate use of skills and processes at a preestablished level.

This is exactly what the AHP attempts. In partnership with its 15 national affiliates, American Humanics has identified the skills and processes for entry-level youth workers and human service work in nonprofit organizations. These competencies are grouped as follows:

I. Foundations for youth and human services nonprofit management
- Career development and exploration
- Communication skills
- Employability skills
- Personal attributes
- Historical and philosophical foundations
- Youth and adult development

II. Professional development: Youth and human services nonprofit management
- Board/committee development
- Fundraising principles and practices
- Human resource development and supervision
- General nonprofit management
- Nonprofit accounting and financial management

- Program planning
- Risk management

As Patterson and Vitello (1994) point out, certification does not necessarily ensure professionalism because professionalism is defined as the "qualities or skills of a profession or professionals." Their view is that skills are competencies and that qualities are characteristics such as integrity. Certification sets the standards of practice, and professionalism defines the manner in which individuals carry out their roles and responsibilities related to job competencies. The 20 campus AHP programs combine an emphasis on skills and knowledge with an emphasis on attitude and values. American Humanics programs identify students with a mission orientation and affirm in students the importance of nonprofit work so that the students have a passion for the work of the nonprofit with which they connect. In regard to current trends in credentialing and certification, American Humanics is in the forefront and may be a pacesetter.

Majors and Minors

The Carnegie Foundation for the Advancement of Teaching (1977) concluded that the major in colleges and universities appears healthy and at many institutions serves as the source of social contacts, personal advice, and the focus of undergraduate life. To keep the major in perspective, the foundation recommended the development of two major options in each department, one option for students intending to pursue graduate school and one for other students. Levine (1978) points out that this particularly applies to the arts and sciences because only 43 percent of undergraduates responding to the undergraduate survey by the Carnegie Council on Policy Studies in Higher Education in 1976 indicated that they were going to graduate school.

Schools such as Arizona State University or Lindenwood College have integrated the AHP into their respective majors and thus provide students with preparation for graduate school or ready entry into the job market. The certification prepares students for the job market. It is competency-driven and has been developed by nonprofits looking to AHP schools such as ASU. As for graduate school preparation, any good department should adequately train its graduates to pursue graduate work. Whether by design or happenstance, ASU, Lindenwood College, and others like them utilizing the AHP as part of a major are following the recommendations of Levine (1978).

Offering a minor is indicated by Levine (1978, pp. 36–37) as making students more employable upon graduation. In fact, Levine notes that some colleges and universities are creating minors, especially for liberal arts students, to specifically increase employability. The American Humanics certificate does this whether it is called a minor or a certificate program.

Gaff (1991), in assessing further educational reform in higher education, notes an innovative program at Wheaton College that assists senior liberal arts students to become more familiar with the world of work. Whether within a major, as a minor, or in a certification program, American Humanics is explicitly training youth and human service nonprofit professionals. The American Humanics philosophy and competencies emphasize the de facto uncertainty, variability, and complexity identified by Lawson (1990) as most important to prepare students for work in the postmodern world.

Experiential Education

Experiential education involves not merely observing the phenomenon being studied but also doing something with the phenomenon, such as testing the dynamics of reality or applying the theory learned. Experiential learning is not just "offcampus" or "nonclassroom learning" but might consist of student practice on critical thinking problems rather than conducting the class entirely by lecture (Keeton and Tate, 1978). Experiential learning dates back before "clinical experiences" for medical students in the 1870s and "applied studies" in post–Civil War era land-grant institutions. By the 1980s over 70 percent of colleges and universities had experiential programs in their curricula, according to Dudley and Permaul (1984). They identified several reasons for the sharp growth of experiential education in recent years: egalitarian values, learning to cope with real-world situations, and applying knowledge. They believe that experiential education causes students to apply knowledge from the classroom and develop action-oriented skills. It enriches the curriculum and establishes a collaboration with the larger community, demystifying the "ivory tower" among "town folk." Potential implications for institutions are multifaceted and include improved financial and political support as well as increased employment opportunities for graduates. This is certainly true for American Humanics programs and their campuses.

American Humanics programs emphasize experiential learning; this is seen most clearly in the minimum 300-hour internship requirement. Internships have an extremely positive influence on employers (Avis and Trice, 1991). As Bruce (1993) points out, most college graduates can say that "they know this or that"; but students who have done an internship can say, "I have done this." Organizations prefer hiring college graduates who understand their operations and corporate culture and who can contribute to the organization immediately. American Humanics programs emphasize experiential learning in classroom experiences, in co-curricular activities of the student organization, and through the internship requirement for certification. Again, the AHP positions its campuses at the forefront of current trends in college and university instruction.

UNDERGRADUATE PROGRAMS AND THE TRAINING OF NONPROFIT PROFESSIONALS

Our conclusion is that the AHP provides a strong case for undergraduate training of nonprofit professionals. The fact that 15 of the largest nonprofit organizations in the United States look to the AHP as a major source to fill 10,000 entry-level positions a year strongly reinforces our conclusion. Also reinforcing our conclusion is the fact that the 15 supporting nonprofits collaborated in establishing the competencies for certification and the role that the teaching of values and attitudes has in the program. From the vantage point of colleges and universities that train teachers, chemists, accountants, and other professionals at the undergraduate level, American Humanics provides a nationally recognized certificate with a rationale for the skills, knowledge, and experience leading to the certification. American Humanics positions its programs and institutions on the forefront of curricular advances and teaching techniques. The program establishes an important and intrinsic relationship between undergraduate education programs at colleges and universities and nonprofit organizations. American Humanics would never maintain that graduate training in nonprofit management/administration is inappropriate. Graduate training in nonprofit management/administration should exist for the more advanced training of supervisors, directors, and executive directors. The role of American Humanics and undergraduate curriculums in the training of entry-level professionals is replacing the time-honored tradition of hiring anyone with a college degree and having nonprofits provide them on-the-job training. This often leads to high turnover as entrants discover the match is not good. American Humanics attempts to make this process more efficient. While any specifically designed undergraduate program might do this, American Humanics is the only current national level program specifically so designed.

APPENDIX 7.1
INDICES ON ASPECTS OF AMERICAN HUMANICS PROGRAMS

For all items of the five indexes, respondents were assigned numerical scores from 1 to 5 depending on whether they answered "strongly agree," "agree," "undecided," "disagree," or "strongly disagree."

Employment Success Index:
1.   I feel that American Humanics enhances my job prospects upon graduation.
2.   American Humanics courses are directly related to employment after graduation.
3.   Competencies of the American Humanics Program are desired by employers.

Expectation Index:
1.   I hoped the American Humanics program would give me information on working in the nonprofit sector.
2.   I hoped the American Humanics program would teach me about volunteer management.
3.   I hoped the American Humanics program would teach me about not-for-profit accounting.
4.   I hoped the American Humanics program would teach me about organizational behavior.
5.   I hoped the American Humanics program would teach me about fundraising.
6.   I hoped the American Humanics program would enable me to find employment in the nonprofit sector.

Knowledge Gained Index:
1.   The American Humanics curriculum allowed me to learn more about myself as a person.
2.   The American Humanics curriculum allowed me to learn more about my capabilities.
3.   The American Humanics curriculum provided me information on the not-for-profit sector.
4.   The American Humanics curriculum taught me about volunteer management.
5.   The American Humanics curriculum taught me about management.
6.   The American Humanics curriculum taught me about nonprofit accounting.
7.   The American Humanics curriculum taught me about fund raising.
8.   The American Humanics curriculum has taught me how to interview for jobs in the nonprofit sector.

Positive Aspects Index:
1.   My American Humanics professors take a personal interest in my success.
2.   A sense of direction and purpose for my studies is an outcome of the American Humanics Program.
3.   Meaningful friendships with students have resulted from my participation in American Humanics.
4.   American Humanics activities are relevant.

5.   Contact with agency professionals is a positive aspect of American Humanics.
6.   Volunteering to work in not-for-profit organizations is a valuable experience
     for future employment.

Usefulness Index:
1.   American Humanics courses focus on useful information.
2.   American Humanics courses focus on useful skills.
3.   American Humanics courses teach useful techniques.

8

Higher Education in Volunteer Administration: Exploring—and Critiquing—the State of the Art

Jeffrey L. Brudney and Gretchen E. Stringer

Volunteers are crucial to the maintenance and performance of a thriving nonprofit sector. Indeed, some titles for the sector, such as the "voluntary sector," make explicit the linkage between volunteers and the health of nonprofit organizations. Many nonprofit agencies are vitally dependent on volunteers for assistance in service delivery, support of paid staff, and fundraising. According to national surveys commissioned by Independent Sector, about 70 percent of all volunteer labor is directed to nonprofit organizations (Hodgkinson, Weitzman, Abrahams, Crutchfield, and Stevenson, 1996, p. 105). Almost all of the remainder benefits government organizations, for example, public schools, youth development activities, and culture and arts institutions such as museums. The literature also celebrates the policy-making and governance role played by volunteers on the boards of directors of nonprofit organizations. For many nonprofit organizations, administering nonpaid, voluntary personnel is a large and exacting aspect of the management task.

Despite the importance of volunteer administration to the nonprofit sector (and governmental sector), precise data do not exist on the number of people whose responsibilities include the management of volunteers. Several factors lie behind this gap. Administrators of volunteers work in a very wide array of organizations and jobs. Few of them perform volunteer administration exclusively; most have other mainline job responsibilities (Brudney, 1990). In addition, the formal job titles assigned to them often mask the connection to volunteers. Volunteerism expert Ivan Scheier (1997) is aware of "at least a dozen job titles under which people work as directors of volunteer programs." "Human resources manager," "personnel administrator," and "director of community services" are common titles, but the position may also be housed in the public relations or marketing departments in larger organizations and in the office of the executive director (or her or his assistant) in smaller ones.

These difficulties notwithstanding, the total number of people engaged in volunteer administration is undoubtedly substantial. The Association for Volunteer Administration (AVA), the largest member organization in this field, uses an estimate of 50,000. Based on surveys of local associations called "Directors of Volunteers in Agencies" (DOVIAs), Scheier (1997) has produced an estimate of at least 100,000 people who coordinate the activities of volunteers. Another expert in the field, Susan Ellis (1997), places the number at 200,000. These projections of size of the volunteer administration workforce do not seem unreasonable. Estimates of the population of nonprofit organizations employing paid staff are about two million, and the total number of voluntary groups, associations, and nonprofit organizations in the United States (with paid staff or not) is estimated to be about 9.5 million (Smith, 1997, p. 119).

While volunteer administration has existed as long as have nonprofit organizations, movement toward a profession is a more recent development (Fisher and Cole, 1993). The difficulties in identifying practitioners in the field, as described earlier, have been an impediment. AVA began in 1960 as the "American Association of Volunteer Services Coordinators." The mission of AVA "is to shape the future of volunteerism, locally, nationally, and internationally, by promoting and strengthening the profession of volunteer services management" (Association for Volunteer Administration, 1995). Toward this end, AVA has promulgated a *Statement of Professional Ethics in Volunteer Administration*, sponsors a quarterly journal (*The Journal of Volunteer Administration*) and other publications, and holds yearly training conferences. Since 1967, AVA has awarded a performance-based credential, "Certified in Volunteer Administration" (CVA), to members who demonstrate proficiency in a set of competencies essential to successful volunteer management. In 1997 AVA had about 1,300 members.

The purpose of this chapter is to determine the extent to which academic programs specializing in nonprofit management prepare graduates for the important task of working with volunteer personnel. Based on a survey of academic programs in this domain, the study assesses the degree of coverage of volunteer administration and management in the curriculum. The study obtained information not only from the preeminent institutions for research and education on the nonprofit sector but also from a sample of academic programs that, while not generally known for a concentration on nonprofit organizations, maintain an emphasis or focus on volunteerism. Prior research has not considered the issue of coverage of the topic of volunteer administration and management in higher education curricula.

BACKGROUND

Lester Salamon (1992, p. 5) points out that the term "voluntary sector" is sometimes used to designate the nonprofit world, because it "emphasizes the significant input that volunteers make to the management and operation of this sector." He considers "voluntary" one of the six defining characteristics of nonprofit organizations, for these entities involve some meaningful degree of voluntary participation, either in the actual conduct of the agency's activities or in the management of its affairs. Often, he explains, participation takes the form of a voluntary board of directors, "but extensive use of volunteer staff is also common" (Salamon, 1992, pp. 6–7). Similarly, Robert D. Herman and Richard D. Heimovics (1990, p. 167) consider the "extent of reliance on volunteers for program delivery" as one of the chief characteristics differentiating nonprofit organizations from business firms and government agencies. Michael O'Neill (1990, p. 206) shares this perspective (compare O'Neill and Young, 1988, p. 3).

Brian O'Connell (1981, p. 29) is more emphatic. In delineating the functions of volunteers and paid staff in voluntary agencies, he observes that the primary job of staff "is to bring about the maximum *volunteer* dedication, *volunteer* involvement, *volunteer* responsibility, *volunteer* impact and *volunteer* satisfaction" (emphasis in the original). Although O'Connell's view is idealized and cannot apply with equal force to the diversity of institutions characterizing the nonprofit sector so well documented by scholars such as Salamon (1992) and O'Neill (1989), the field endorses unequivocally the significant involvement of volunteers in nonprofit organizations.

The National Clarion Conference convened in 1989 to address some of the fundamental instructional questions involved in developing an academic field of nonprofit administration (Rubin, Adamski, and Block, 1989). This conference, too, gave strong rhetorical support to a focus on volunteerism (pp. 282–284). Yet, although the model for instruction in nonprofit administration emanating from the conference included "board and volunteer development and management" as one of the skill areas, the topic received only passing mention (p. 285). Similarly, a major edited volume on nonprofit management education recognizes the importance and distinctiveness of volunteer involvement for the sector but does not devote serious attention to instruction in the administration and management of nonpaid personnel (O'Neill and Young, 1988). The present research considers the extent of coverage of this topic that has evolved in the curricula of academic programs in nonprofit organization management.

RESEARCH METHODS

To address these issues, the authors developed a three-page survey concerned with educational practices of nonprofit academic degree programs for teaching about volunteer administration and management. The survey was administered by mail, with a return-postage-paid envelope provided.

Sampling Frame and Response

As other researchers have discovered, assembling a sampling frame of academic programs in nonprofit organization management for dissemination of the survey proved no easy matter. The researchers relied on several means.

We mailed the questionnaire to all institutions of higher learning identified on Independent Sector's listing of "Academic Centers and Programs Focusing on the Study of Philanthropy, Voluntarism and Nonprofit Activities" (as of October 1995). The listing encompasses the premiere institutions with educational degree programs and research centers in this domain. We supplemented this sample in several ways; first, with a 1995 listing provided by Naomi Bailin Wish and colleagues at Seton Hall University of "Universities Offering Graduate Programs in Nonprofit Management." Although this listing overlaps substantially with that provided by Independent Sector, it includes additional nonprofit educational degree programs. We also sent the questionnaire to all members of the Association for Volunteer Administration (AVA) Subcommittee on Volunteer Administration in Higher Education, which consists of approximately 175 members. The subcommittee includes both AVA members and nonmembers who have an interest in educational programs in volunteer administration and/or nonprofit management. We anticipated that at least some of these individuals would be affiliated with institutions offering degree programs in these or related fields. Finally, at the 1995 annual meetings of both AVA and the Association for Research on Nonprofit Organizations and Voluntary Action (ARNOVA), we distributed a handful of surveys to representatives of schools with a nonprofit program or concentration whose institutions had appeared on none of these listings.

The initial mailing of the questionnaire and one follow-up mailing to nonrespondents, plus repeated telephone requests to schools on the Independent Sector and Seton Hall mailing lists that had not responded, yielded a total sample of 80 academic degree programs. We concentrated on these two listings because they encompass the leading academic programs in nonprofit organization management (the lists overlap significantly). In addition, most of the members of the AVA Subcommittee on Volunteer Administration in Higher Education are practitioners in the nonprofit sector, rather than teaching faculty. The sample includes 32 of the 38 institutions identified by Independent Sector and another seven programs identified by the Seton Hall researchers (but not appearing on the Independent Sector listing).

Academic Programs in the Sample

Appendix 8.1 shows the academic programs that responded to the survey regarding educational practices in volunteer administration and management and the respective listing on which the institution had appeared (that is, the roster provided by Independent Sector, Seton Hall, or AVA). All major institutions for the study of the nonprofit sector are represented. For example, included in the sample are the main academic centers and research institutes for the study of nonprofit organizations at Case Western Reserve University, Duke University, Indiana University/Purdue University at Indianapolis, Johns Hopkins University, London School of Economics and Political Science, New School for Social Research, Seton Hall University, Tufts University, University of Missouri-Kansas City, University of San Francisco, Yale University, and York University (Canada).

Examination of the six institutions on the Independent Sector roster that failed to respond to the survey is also revealing. One is Queensland University of Technology, Program on Nonprofit Organizations, in Brisbane, Australia. Distance certainly worked against a response, even though a universal postage-paid voucher for international mail was included with the survey (the Nonprofit Organization Program at the University of Stockholm, Sweden, did respond). The other five programs are in the United States. Repeated telephone calls to these institutions either failed to identify a person responsible for the nonprofit program or ended in a fruitless trail of voice mail. At several of the schools, this position had turned over, and the program appeared to be in disarray. The relative frequency of this occurrence hints at the fragility of academic concentrations in nonprofit organization management. The nonprofit "program" may have been sustained by the interest of a single faculty member in the sector; should that person leave the institution, the program becomes vulnerable and tends to wither. The questionnaire returned by the Center for Volunteer Development at Virginia Polytechnic Institute and State University (listed on the Independent Sector roster) indicated that this program had disbanded. One other institution in the sample reported that the nonprofit program was no longer offered.

In all, 80 completed questionnaires were received from institutions in four countries, predominantly the United States ($N = 69$, or 86 percent) but also Canada ($N = 9$, or 11.3 percent); AVA boasts a substantial membership in Canada. The two remaining surveys were from England (London School of Economics) and Sweden (Nonprofit Organization Program, University of Stockholm).

Table 8.1 describes the types of academic programs in the sample of institutions. As the table shows, 10 programs do not offer academic courses or a degree (primarily research institutes), and another pair of programs have been disbanded (as noted above). When these programs have been excluded from the analysis, about 30 percent of the sample are solely graduate programs. Nearly as many programs, 22 percent, offer a certificate; almost all of the certificates are in volunteer administration, with but a few in nonprofit administration (or both). Undergraduate programs constitute only about 8 percent of the total. Many of the academic programs offer a combination of degrees (graduate and certificate, for example). With combinations taken into account, two-thirds of the sample of institutions grant a graduate degree, and half offer a certificate.

Five of the programs in the sample offer a master's degree in nonprofit organization or management (7.4 percent of the degree-granting institutions). Table 8.2 shows that the master of public administration or policy appears most frequently in the sample (37 percent of programs offer this degree). Certificate programs are next in frequency (23 percent), followed by the master of business administration (9.3 percent).

FINDINGS

The primary goal of the study was to determine the extent to which academic programs with a focus on nonprofit organization management include treatment of volunteer administration and management in the curriculum. The survey asked several questions toward this purpose.

Course Coverage of Volunteer Administration and Management

Responses to the survey indicate that just 23 institutions in the total sample (28.8 percent) offer a course in volunteer administration and management. Two other programs wrote that they used to offer such a course but no longer do so as a consequence of lack of funding or enrollment. When the 12 institutions that do not grant a degree are excluded from consideration, one-third of the sample (33.8 percent) has a course in volunteer administration or management. The survey also asked whether the educational institution offered other courses not specifically directed to volunteer administration and management, but where this subject might receive coverage nonetheless. Here, the responses are more encouraging: 52.5 percent of the total sample (N = 42), or 61.8 percent of those with academic degree programs, give at least some coverage to the topic.

Table 8.1
Type of Degree Program of Institutions in the Sample*

Degree Offered	Total Sample (N = 79)	Educational Degree Programs (N = 67)
Undergraduate	5 (6.3%)	5 (7.5%)
Graduate	20 (25.3%)	20 (29.9%)
Certificate	15 (19.0%)	15 (22.4%)
Undergraduate and graduate	8 (10.1%)	8 (11.9%)
Undergraduate and certificate	1 (1.3%)	1 (1.5%)
Graduate and certificate	13 (16.5%)	13 (19.4%)
Undergraduate, graduate, and certificate	5 (6.3%)	5 (7.5%)
No educational degree program	10 (12.7%)	—
Program disbanded	2 (2.5%)	—

* One program did not supply the information used in this table.

Combining the responses to these two questions yields a more complete picture of the extent of coverage of volunteer administration and management in the curricula of the academic degree programs. About three-fourths of the sample (73.5 percent) feature at least some coverage of this topic through coursework: eight programs (11.8 percent) have a course in the subject but do not cover it further; 27 programs (39.7 percent) do not have a dedicated course but provide some exposure to volunteer administration and management in a different course; 15 programs (22.1 percent) do both. The remaining 18 programs (26.5 percent), however, have no coverage of volunteer administration and management through their curricula.

Course Coverage by Type of Academic Program

Table 8.3 shows how course coverage of the topic of volunteer administration and management differs by type of academic program. The table categorizes the institutions in the sample into two groups: (1) those identified by Independent Sector (N = 25) or the Seton Hall researchers (N = 7) as having a degree program or concentration in nonprofit organization or management and (2) those emanating from the sample of Association of Volunteer Administration members (N = 30) or other sources ($N = 6$). (See Appendix 8.1 for detailed information on the composition of the sample.)

Table 8.2
Name of Academic Degree*

Name of Degree	Institutions Offering This Degree ($N = 67$)
Master of public administration or public policy	24 (35.8%)
Certificate in volunteer or nonprofit administration	15 (22.4%)
Master of business administration	7 (10.4%)
Master of nonprofit organization or management	5 (7.5%)
Other	16 (23.9%)

* One program did not supply the information used in this table.

The first category encompasses the preeminent programs for study of the nonprofit sector, including all schools that offer a master's degree in this field. These programs are the ones that academic advisors would be expected to recommend to promising undergraduates with an interest in graduate education in nonprofit organization management; many of the schools have established research reputations in this area. For convenience, this group is referred to as "Nonprofit Programs." The programs in the second category do not have this distinction and are much more diverse. This group consists predominantly of schools known much less, if at all, for study of the nonprofit sector. Most of these schools have a concentration or emphasis on volunteerism; for example, all programs in the sample that offer certificates only (almost always in volunteer administration with a few in nonprofit management) are in this group. A few other schools in this category have a nonprofit concentration within a master's degree program. In Table 8.3 and thereafter, these schools are labeled "Volunteerism Programs."

According to the results in Table 8.3, the Nonprofit Programs identified by Independent Sector and/or the Seton Hall researchers do not devote great attention through the curriculum to volunteer administration and management. About 30 percent of these schools have no coverage of this field in coursework, and more than half provide coverage only through exposure in other courses (see later discussion for extent of coverage). In all, only four of the 32 schools in this category have a course on the topic (whether supplemented or not through coverage in other courses). The second group of Volunteerism Programs, less known for study or research in nonprofit organizations, provides much greater coverage. More than half of these institutions offer a dedicated course on volunteer administration and management, and 31 percent supplement this course with further coverage in other course(s). Only one quarter of the schools in this group provide coverage of this topic solely through exposure in other courses. Closer analysis of the eight institutions in this group that indicated that they do not offer coverage of volunteer administration and management reveals that these programs are nonprofit concentrations within MBA or MPA programs, rather than programs with a focus on volunteer administration.

Table 8.3
Coverage of Volunteer Administration and Management in the Curriculum

Coverage	Nonprofit Programs (N = 32)	Volunteerism Programs (N = 36)	All Programs (N = 68)
Dedicated course in volunteer administration or management (no other coverage of topic)	0 (0.0%)	8 (22.2%)	8 (11.8%)
Coverage of volunteer administration or management in other course(s) only	18 (56.3%)	9 (25.0%)	27 (39.7%)
Coverage in dedicated course and other course(s)	4 (12.5%)	11 (30.6%)	15 (22.1%)
No coverage of volunteer administration or management	10 (31.3%)	8 (22.2%)	18 (26.5%)

Amount of Coverage in Other Courses

Table 8.4 explores how the amount of coverage of volunteer administration and management in these other courses varies by type of academic program. For this purpose, the questionnaire had asked respondents (1) to list any courses with a different focus that would still deal with aspects of volunteer administration and management and (2) to indicate the total number of contact hours for the course as well as the number of hours devoted to this topic. A respondent could list up to three other courses. For each course, the amount of coverage is calculated as the percentage of course contact hours spent on volunteer administration and management. Table 8.4 presents both the mean and median percentage of coverage in the Nonprofit Programs, the Volunteerism Programs, and all programs. Because the mean values are skewed by the presence of a few outliers with especially high levels of coverage (many of the Volunteerism Programs have several courses in which the topic of volunteer administration and management receives priority), the median values are probably the preferred statistic.

As did Table 8.3, Table 8.4 shows that the subject of volunteer administration and management appears to be covered less thoroughly in the Nonprofit Programs than in the Volunteerism Programs. In all three other courses in which the topic receives some attention, the median level of coverage for the latter group surpasses that in the former group. Moreover, if the mean values are used as the basis for comparison, T tests indicate that the difference in the amount of coverage in all three classes is greater than what would be expected by chance (the null hypothesis of no difference in coverage by degree program can be rejected at conventional levels of statistical significance). Perhaps more important, the median values suggest that, in the other courses, coverage of volunteer administration and management is not great among the Nonprofit Programs; these courses devote only about 11 percent of contact hours to the topic (the equivalent of one or one and one-half lectures in an academic term). In the Volunteerism Programs, the median values suggest roughly twice this amount of coverage.

Responses from the survey indicate that when the topic of volunteer administration and management receives coverage through "other courses" rather than in a dedicated course, a variety of classes may provide the treatment. As might be expected, in the Nonprofit Programs the other courses that tend to touch on the topic most often are "Introduction to the Nonprofit Sector" or "Management of Nonprofit Organizations" (or courses with similar titles such as "Topics in Nonprofit Management" or "Nonprofit Administration"). More specialized courses dealing with the nonprofit sector sometimes include coverage, for example, "Fundraising (or Development) for Nonprofit Organizations," "Nonprofit Marketing," "Board Leadership (or Governance) and Development," "Nonprofit Leadership and Decision Making" (or "Strategic Management in Nonprofit Organizations"). Finally, some very general-purpose courses occasionally provide coverage of volunteer administration and management, especially "Human Resource Management" (or "Personnel Administration"), "Human Relations," "Program Development and Evaluation," "Organization Management" (or "Topics in Organization Management"), "Community Development," "Human (or Community) Service Delivery," and "Arts Management."

DISCUSSION

Volunteers are a cornerstone of the nonprofit sector. Symbolically and practically they are at its core. The purpose of this study was to determine whether students with a serious interest in education in nonprofit organization management are receiving through the curricula of academic programs in this field the depth of exposure to volunteer administration and management commensurate with the status and importance of volunteers. To address this issue, the authors prepared and administered a survey to a large sample of academic programs with a focus on nonprofit organizations and/or volunteerism. Featured in the sample are all major programs with this emphasis identified by Independent Sector or researchers at Seton Hall University.

Findings from the survey reveal that, despite the essential role of volunteers to the nonprofit sector, the topic of volunteer administration and management receives only weak coverage in the curriculum of the Nonprofit Programs. About one-third of these institutions seem to ignore this topic in coursework, and more than half provide coverage only through secondary treatment in other courses (that is, courses on a different topic that spend some class time on volunteer administration and management). In these other courses, too, the extent of coverage is not impressive, typically amounting to about 11 percent of class contact hours.

These findings suggest a marked gap in the formal education of aspiring managers and leaders of the nonprofit sector. In the premiere institutions for the study of nonprofit organization management, it is entirely possible, if not likely, that students can graduate from degree programs or complete concentrations without exposure through the curriculum to the topic of volunteer administration and management. For a substantial number of students, just a lecture or two on the topic will have to suffice as preparation for the challenges and problems they may encounter in the nonprofit workplace in administering and managing volunteer workers. In sum, despite extensive rhetorical support for the importance of volunteers to the sector, the major educational degree programs in nonprofit organization management and leadership appear to be doing relatively little to prepare their graduates for working with nonpaid workers.

Another group of approximately one-half of the academic degree programs in the sample provide much greater coverage of volunteer administration and management in the curriculum. Identified by members of the Association for Volunteer Administration Subcommittee on Volunteer Administration in Higher Education, these schools generally do not enjoy a strong reputation for study or research in the nonprofit sector but maintain an emphasis or concentration on volunteerism, for example, certificate programs in volunteer administration.

Table 8.4
Amount of Coverage of Volunteer Administration and Management in Other Courses

Course	Nonprofit Programs			Volunteerism Programs			All Programs		
	Mean %	Median %	N	Mean %	Median %	N	Mean %	Median %	N
1	15.7	11.1	21	44.8	17.8	15	27.8	13.1	36
2	19.4	12.5	13	50.9	40.0	12	34.5	15.0	25
3	12.0	10.4	4	44.6	17.8	8	33.7	12.4	12

Note: Table reports mean and median percentage of course contact hours devoted to volunteer administration and management. Course 1 refers to first course listed by respondent, Course 2 to second course listed, and Course 3 to the third.

In comparison to the Nonprofit Programs, these "Volunteerism Programs" have dedicated courses on volunteer administration and management in the curriculum more often and treat the topic more fully in other courses.

If the leaders of nonprofit educational degree programs want to move in the direction of greater coverage of volunteer administration, the requisite tools for instruction appear to be well within reach. As noted previously, the present research found 23 schools that offer a course on volunteer administration and management, and a previous study by Stringer (1993) uncovered a longer list of institutions. Obtaining syllabi as a starting point for new course development or for integration of this material into related courses should not prove difficult. The survey administered as part of the present study also solicited the names of books that have been used as texts in courses on volunteer administration and management. According to the survey responses, suitable books are available, including works by Fisher and Cole (1993), McCurley and Lynch (1989), and Brudney (1990).

While these instructional tools could facilitate greater integration of volunteer administration and management into the curricula of nonprofit management programs, educators will also confront inhibitors. Perhaps chief among them is the relative "invisibility" of volunteer administration as a profession. As discussed at the outset of this chapter, despite the ubiquity of volunteers in the nonprofit sector and the work of the many thousands of people whose job entails coordinating and directing the activities of volunteers, the field has not gained recognition commensurate with the qualifications for the job or the "value added" it brings to organizations in the form of donated labor, expertise, vitality, and community support. In many nonprofit organizations, locating the official with responsibility for the volunteers either on the organization chart or in the operations of the agency can pose quite a challenge: Job titles cannot be trusted to convey the relationship to volunteers, and the position usually encompasses other important duties. In nonprofit organizations, too, directors of volunteer services tend to receive less monetary compensation than other occupations and, according to surveys of practitioners, are given less respect (Brudney, 1992). These factors will likely not be lost on students seeking careers in the nonprofit sector and may depress classroom enrollments. In an analogous manner, the academic community has not concentrated great attention on the position or the profession; comparatively little research has addressed the director of volunteer services (Brudney and Kluesner, 1992).

With relatively few schools offering courses on volunteer administration and few faculty having had access to them, leaders of nonprofit programs desiring greater coverage of this field in the curriculum might consider the use of thoughtful practitioners in the classroom. The fusion of academic knowledge and practical training has much to recommend it and may, in fact, be on the cutting edge of nonprofit studies. Carl Milofsky (1996, p. 282) writes that eminent scholars "seem to envision a melding of practical and intellectual knowledge in which the world of practice and the world of the academy mutually inform each other." Milofsky cautions that "this does not reflect a familiar academic scene" and that the meaning and parameters of such a fusion have yet to be settled. For those nonprofit programs with an interest, more prosaic options are also possible, for instance, insuring that volunteer administration and management are treated as a core topic in courses on human resource management.

CONCLUSION

A larger issue than the means by which volunteer administration and management might be introduced into the curriculum of the nonprofit programs or given greater coverage is the commitment of program leaders to instruction in this domain. The fact that the topic of volunteer administration and management rarely commands a course of its own or substantial coverage in other courses in the nonprofit programs sends a very definite signal regarding its perceived relevance and significance. Research beyond the scope of the present study is necessary and important to determine the courses that do appear in the curricula of these programs and how these classes might contribute to satisfying, productive careers of students in nonprofit organizations. For a sector that builds and prides itself on the spirit, caring, and labor of nonpaid citizens, however, it is difficult to rationalize how understanding and appreciation of the issues and demands of working with volunteers could be any less crucial than the subjects now covered in the curricula of the major nonprofit programs.

APPENDIX 8.1
INSTITUTIONS OF HIGHER LEARNING RESPONDING TO THE
SURVEY

NAME OF COLLEGE OR UNIVERSITY	CITY, STATE (COUNTRY)
American University (Master of Arts Management)	Washington, DC
American University (Master of Public Administration)	Washington, DC
Arizona State University	Tempe, Arizona
Boston College*	Boston, Massachusetts
California State University (Hayward)	Hayward, California
Carleton College	Northfield, Minnesota
Case Western Reserve University (Mandel Center)*	Cleveland, Ohio
City University of New York (Graduate School and University Center)*	New York, New York
Des Moines Area Community College (Certificate in Volunteer Management)	Des Moines, Iowa
Duke University (Certificate in Non-Profit Management)	Durham, North Carolina
Duke University (Master of Public Policy)*	Durham, North Carolina
Durham College	Oshawa, Ontario (Canada)
George Brown College	Toronto, Ontario (Canada)
George Mason University*	Arlington, Virginia
George Washington University+	Washington, DC
Georgia State University+	Atlanta, Georgia
Georgian College of Applied Arts and Technology (Certificate—non-credit)	Edmonton, Alberta (Canada)
Grand Valley State University*	Grand Rapids, Michigan
Grant MacEwan Community College (Certificate in Non-Profit Agency Management)	Superman City, Alberta (Canada)
Harvard University (Kennedy School)*	Cambridge, Massachusetts
Hilbert College	Buffalo, New York
Illinois Wesleyan University	Bloomington, Illinois
Indiana University (Diploma in Philanthropic Studies)*	Indianapolis, Indiana
Indiana University	Bloomington, Indiana
Indiana University (School of Business)	Bloomington, Indiana
Johns Hopkins University*	Baltimore, Maryland

Laurentian University (National certification program in Volunteer and Non-Profit Sector Management)	Sudbury, Ontario (Canada)
Lewis and Clark College (Institute for Nonprofit Management)	Portland, Oregon
Lincoln Land Community College	Springfield, Illinois
London School of Economics*	London, England
Marywood College*	Scranton, Pennsylvania
Metro State University	Minneapolis, Minnesota
Mohawk College	Hamilton, Ontario (Canada)
National Center for Nonprofit Boards*	Washington, DC
National Louis University	Evanston, Illinois
National Louis University	Chicago, Illinois
New School for Social Research*	New York, New York
New York University*	New York, New York
New York University (School of Law)*	New York, New York
Ohio State University	Columbus, Ohio
Pepperdine University	Malibu, California
Rockefeller Archive Center*	Westchester, New York
Rockhurst College (Certificate in American Humanics)	Kansas City, Missouri
Roosevelt University (Certificate in Nonprofit Management)+	Chicago, Illinois
Seattle University	Seattle, Washington
Seton Hall University*	South Orange, New Jersey
Southern Methodist University*	Dallas, Texas
Stockholm University (School of Business)*	Stockholm (Sweden)
St. Clair College of Applied Arts and Technology (Volunteer Management Certificate)	Edmonton, Alberta (Canada)
Texas Christian University*	Fort Worth, Texas
Texas Tech University	Lubbock, Texas
Tufts University (Certificate in Community Organization Management)*	Medford, Massachusetts
Union Institute (Certificate in Management of Volunteers)*	Cincinnati, Ohio
University of Alabama at Birmingham+	Birmingham, Alabama
University of Arizona	Tucson, Arizona
University of California at Berkeley*	Berkeley, California
University of California at San Francisco (Institute for Health and Aging)*	San Francisco, California
University of California at Santa Barbara	Santa Barbara, California
University of Chicago (Harris Graduate School)+	Chicago, Illinois

University of Colorado at Colorado Springs+   Colorado Springs,
                                                                              Colorado

University of Maryland (University College)*   College Park, Maryland
University of Memphis   Memphis, Tennessee
University of Missouri at Kansas City*   Kansas City, Missouri
University of New Hampshire   Portsmouth,
                                                                              New Hampshire

University of Oklahoma   Norman, Oklahoma
University of Pittsburgh (Certificate in Nonprofit
  Management)+   Pittsburgh,
                                                                              Pennsylvania

University of San Francisco (Certificate in
  Nonprofit Management)*   San Francisco,
                                                                              California

University of Southern Maine (Certificate in
  Volunteer Management)   Portland, Maine
University of St. Thomas*   Minneapolis, Minnesota
University of Texas at Arlington   Arlington, Texas
University of Texas at Pan American   Edinberg, Texas
University of Utah   Salt Lake City , Utah
University of Wisconsin at Madison (Center For
  Women and Philanthropy)*   Madison, Wisconsin
Virginia Polytechnic Institute and State
  University*   Blacksburg, Virginia
West Virginia University   Morgantown,
                                                                              West Virginia

Western Piedmont Community College   Hickory, North Carolina
William Rainey Harper College (Certificate in
  Volunteer Management)   Palatine, Illinois
Yale University*   New Haven,
                                                                              Connecticut

York University (Certificate in Volunteer Sector
  Management)*   Toronto, Ontario
                                                                              (Canada)

* Institution identified on the Independent Sector 1995 listing of "Academic Centers and
Programs Focusing on the Study of Philanthropy, Voluntarism and Nonprofit Activities."

+ Institution identified on 1995 Seton Hall University listing of "University-Based Post-
graduate Programs in Nonprofit Management" (but not appearing on the Independent
Sector listing of institutions).

All remaining institutions identified from the 1995 listing provided by the Association
for Volunteer Administration Subcommittee on Volunteer Administration in Higher
Education.

9

Building the Nonprofit Sector Knowledge Base: Can Academic Centers and Management Support Organizations Come Together?

Rick Smith

INTRODUCTION

The purpose of this chapter is twofold: first, to shed light on the important education, training, and research work of management support organizations (MSOs), a relatively new type of community-based organization that is contributing to the knowledge development and research efforts in the field of nonprofit management and, second, to make a case for much greater dialogue and interaction between MSOs and the growing pool of academics and academic centers dedicated to the development of a nonprofit knowledge base and the advancement of nonprofit management.

The chapter summarizes a series of interviews conducted with two sets of nonprofit leaders: those who manage MSOs and those who run management education programs within institutions of higher education. Their names and affiliations are given in Appendix 9.1.

THE MANAGEMENT SUPPORT FIELD: ADVANCING NONPROFIT MANAGEMENT

As the nonprofit sector continues to assume a greater degree of responsibility for society's health and welfare, there is new interest in the care and feeding of the sector. This concern quickly leads to a discussion of the infrastructure that supports charity. Like other major sectors in society, the nonprofit sector relies on an infrastructure of supporting resources to develop and prosper. Today, in the United States alone, there are over a million tax-exempt nonprofit organizations. A tiny fraction of these organizations exist solely to help all the others function well. Each support organization focuses on the coordination and delivery of essential resources—the financial, volunteer, information/knowledge, and management resources—that enable nonprofit organizations to operate effectively. The MSO field is one of several core components that comprise the current infrastructure and is arguably the least studied and understood component. After decades of lukewarm interest by philanthropy, there is evidence that nonprofit leaders are acknowledging the pivotal role of management resources in the larger mix of factors that produces successful nonprofit enterprise. Increasingly, management resources are seen as a strategic resource, as important as both financial and human resources. Without quality management these resources will be underutilized or even wasted. The underlying assumption is that a real link exists between an organization's management capabilities and its effectiveness.

Today, after over 25 years of development and maturation, a young industry comprised of MSOs is devoted to improving the effectiveness of other nonprofit organizations and the people that manage and govern them. With hundreds of MSOs (including dedicated programs housed within an umbrella organization) currently in operation, the MSO industry is firmly rooted in the American nonprofit landscape. The *Survey and Analysis of Management Support Organizations, 1994–95* (Simmons and Szabat, 1996b) developed by the La Salle University Nonprofit Management Development Center (NMDC) presents the most comprehensive data on the MSO field. According to the report, "the typical MSO"

- has a regional service area, serving multiple counties in a geographic area including 3,000 nonprofits;
- provides public training, customized in-house training, information and referral, and consulting services;
- has a paid staff of 4.5 FTEs and a budget of $317,848;
- relies heavily on the use of professional volunteers to deliver services;
- provides its services to a wide variety of nonprofit organizations and mostly to organizations with budgets under $500,000;
- provides assistance in a variety of management areas;
- is independently incorporated (65%);
- was founded in 1979 or 1990;
- charges fees ($50/hr or $65/day for workshop training);
- is increasing its consulting work.

While the stated missions and specific programs of MSOs vary slightly, virtually all are focused on providing management resources to nonprofit organizations with the goal of improving organizational effectiveness. The largest component of this mission involves training and educating nonprofit managers. The MSO field is the single largest management education force operating for the benefit of nonprofit managers (and volunteers). A very conservative estimate suggests that over 250,000 nonprofit managers annually participate in training programs provided by management support organizations. MSOs are also heavily engaged in management consulting and information programs. Together, training, consulting, and information programs comprise the core services of most MSOs.

As the field matures, an increasing number of MSOs are getting involved in research projects. For example, the Support Center for Nonprofit Management in San Francisco, one of the oldest and largest MSOs, recently conducted research on practices and perspectives related to indirect costs and on client experiences with the HIV health services delivery system. Both studies included significant involvement with nonprofit practitioners. In another effort, the Support Centers of America conducted extensive research into its training programs as part of a nationwide evaluation study to better understand its own program effectiveness.

The Nonprofit Management Association (NMA) counts over 500 MSOs in the United States (including established programs within larger organizational umbrellas such as local United Ways and nonprofit statewide associations). The field continues to mature and grow in response to the substantial need in the nonprofit sector. Around the world, various forces are at work promoting the development of the nonprofit or "nongovernmental" sector; it is not surprising that management training and assistance are increasing worldwide.

THE NEED AND OPPORTUNITY FOR PRODUCTIVE DIALOGUE AND INTERACTION BETWEEN ACADEMIC CENTERS AND MSOS

Despite similar missions, programs, interests, and needs, MSOs and academic centers devoted to nonprofit management have largely operated in isolation from one another. The separation represents an enormous missed opportunity for the nonprofit sector and the society it serves. Academic centers and MSOs are natural allies in which the exchange and sharing of resources can produce truly synergistic results.

The similarities between academic centers and MSOs are striking. First, they share a similar mission. Both sets of institutions seek to increase the effectiveness of non-profit management professionals through education and information programs. One person interviewed for this study, Rob Hollister, dean of the Graduate School of Arts and Sciences at Tufts University, commented that MSOs and academic centers "really are in the same business and share the same consumer market." After making a similar point about consumer markets, Michael O'Neill, director of the Institute for Nonprofit Organization Management at the University of San Francisco and one of the pioneers in the nonprofit management education field, described the important influence of a senior MSO practitioner in helping him understand the need for an academic program in nonprofit management.

I got the idea for the Master of Nonprofit Administration program during a conversation with Barbara Schilling at the Management Center [a San Francisco MSO]. I asked her if she thought that such a program would be of interest and value to nonprofit managers; she said, "Very much so." Barbara was a member of the original advisory board of the Institute, which started in 1983. This advisory board played a major role in shaping the curriculum, adjunct faculty list, scheduling, marketing, and other aspects of the program. We continue to work closely with MSOs in Northern California. I feel that the university-MSO relationship has played a centrally important role in the effectiveness of our master's degree and, later, certificate programs for nonprofit leaders.

Most colleges and universities focus, to varying degrees, on three programmatic areas: teaching, research, and community and professional service. MSOs tend to focus their resources on training, direct assistance (consulting), and information (including some research) programs. All these programs seek to enhance the professionalism and management capabilities of nonprofit managers and volunteers.

In addition to program similarity, MSOs and academic centers have an even more compelling basis for collaboration: to build an improved knowledge base that supports the activities and goals of both types of institutions. Good, reliable knowledge underlies everything academic centers and MSOs do. Each and every MSO and academic program is dependent on an accessible and tested knowledge base. Academics, obviously, are more interested in formalizing the knowledge that is developed. Less sensitive to the formal knowledge development process, the MSO profession, nevertheless, has a significant interest in the codification process. Knowledge retrieval and professional development rely heavily on a formal and accessible knowledge platform. Joe Mixer, a cofounder of the Fund Raising School and an adjunct faculty member at the University of California at Berkeley and the University of San Francisco, echoed the widely shared belief that "a knowledge base is one of several critical elements of any true profession."

The shared need for an excellent knowledge base provides an important basis for better collaboration between academic centers and MSOs in the future. Both types of institutions possess complementary resources to contribute to this critically important and ongoing task. MSOs have experience with thousands of nonprofit organizations in the broad range of management disciplines and issues. With contacts and experience throughout a nonprofit community, local MSO professionals represent an invaluable connection to the local nonprofit sector. Further, MSOs typically have aggregated client data, from mailing lists to consumer data, that is regularly collected and stored as part of their services business.

Academic centers bring an equally valuable set of resources to the process of knowledge development. First and foremost, they represent the institutional vehicles that enable individuals with sufficient time, research training, and intellect to pursue formal knowledge development. In addition, there is the continuing institutional commitment to the rigorous pursuit and dissemination of new knowledge.

Professionals in the MSO field are particularly well positioned to help academics understand the actual issues and concerns confronting nonprofit practitioners. Because of their unique position as consultants and trainers with numerous community organizations, MSO practitioners are a repository of practical and "real world" knowledge, acquired through numerous hours of working in organizational laboratories on a daily basis. These individuals have experience with a myriad of managers and volunteer leaders in the full spectrum of management issues and topics. This "hands-on" experience can help academics determine research agendas and frame relevant research questions.

While practitioners are focused on practical, how-to approaches to knowledge, academics have the interest and skills for developing sound theory and conceptual frameworks and providing a deeper understanding of what is really occurring in the field. A profession needs both good theory and sound, practical information regarding behavior, systems, and best practices. Both are necessary for full understanding of the world, and both contribute to enhanced problem-solving for professionals in the field.

Hollister noted that greater collaborative work on research involving both academics and practitioners was bound to produce a "more robust and higher quality of research." As a first step, he suggested that practitioners need to be regularly involved in developing the agenda of future research. Hollister and several additional interviewees praised the efforts of the Aspen Institute Nonprofit Sector Research Fund to sponsor and support practitioner-based research. In a recently published report, *Mission Possible: 200 Ways to Strengthen the Nonprofit Sector's Infrastructure*, the Union Institute echoed these themes with the following strategy recommendation:

Create an organization or use existing organizations to better coordinate work being done by academics and practitioners. Support the notion of "applied research"; increase opportunities for practitioners to hear about and use research findings. Include input from nonprofits on what kinds of research they would find useful; educate nonprofits on data-keeping and use of data. Regional associations of grantmakers (RAGs), community foundations or region-specific MSOs could serve as the locus for such services. (Chieco, Koch, and Scotchmer, 1996, p. 70)

There is a widespread belief that bringing together MSO practitioners and academics could accelerate the utility of knowledge throughout the sector. Nora Silver, director of the Volunteerism Project in San Francisco, commented that there is a need "to compress the knowledge development process by accelerating the pace by which theoretical ideas are tested in laboratory situations." She added that MSOs could be helpful in this process. Jane Arsenault, an independent consultant and former executive director of the Support Center of Rhode Island, suggested that "we need to identify academicians with an interest in real-life applications—scholars who are interested in adding and adapting new knowledge rather than just conveying a body of knowledge." Equally important are practitioners who understand the practical value of good theory and who have a commitment to building a core understanding of the theoretical basis of organizational and human behavior.

A related issue concerns the need to disseminate existing research. Several interviewees suggested that MSOs and academics could work together on translating academic research into user-friendly materials that could be tested and used in the field. As an example of this process, Karen Simmons, executive director of the Nonprofit Management Development Center in Philadelphia, cited the research work of Larry E. Griener at Harvard University on organizational life cycles and its subsequent translation into practitioner-oriented materials by Karl Mathiasen, a founding director of the Management Assistance Group in Washington, D.C.

Another example is Silver's doctoral research on volunteerism in community service organizations, now a book for practitioners titled *At the Heart: The New Volunteer Challenge for Community Agencies* (Silver, 1988). For such efforts to continue, an ongoing process is needed to identify academics and practitioners who have a desire to translate and disseminate new knowledge products.

A good example of the integration of theoretical and practical knowledge can be found in the fund development field. The knowledge and information developed by Henry Rosso and Joe Mixer, the founders of the Fund Raising School, integrates theoretical and practical knowledge. The resulting training curriculum offers students a comprehensive learning experience that goes beyond lengthy descriptions of how-to fundraising tools and techniques. The curriculum and learning experience were designed to give student practitioners the analytic tools to develop situation-specific approaches to a variety of fundraising challenges. According to Mixer, "Practitioners need more than standardized how-to prescriptions—they need the theoretical conceptual framework to excel in real-life problem solving."   Actual problems often demand creative solutions, and these solutions often cannot be uncovered in books and simple case studies.

A major problem is the dearth of professional intersections for academics and MSO practitioners.   More and better dialogue between MSO practitioners and academics needs to occur in the future.   Leaders in both fields need to promote greater attendance at each other's professional conferences—more academics need to attend the Nonprofit Management Association (NMA) conference and MSO practitioners must start attending the annual Association for Research on Nonprofit Organizations and Voluntary Action (ARNOVA) conference.   Interviewees also suggested that specific practitioner-academic discussion forums be organized as a core component of these conferences. Recently, both ARNOVA and NMA have moved in this direction.   For example, at the 1997 NMA conference, a series of "Bridge the Gap" sessions pairing MSO practitioners with academics were held to discuss specific projects that can be implemented in the near future.

In addition, specific new forums like the "Think Tank" conducted at the Indiana University Center on Philanthropy in June 1995 need to be developed. At this session, 38 fundraising practitioners and academic specialists convened to discuss the gulf between fundraising theory and practice. Establishment of such forums that encourage and promote in-depth dialogue is a critical preliminary step in the larger collaborative process.

Joint-venture programming is potentially another major opportunity for MSOs and academic centers to work together productively.   Integrating training and teaching forums to produce symposiums, conferences, and jointly sponsored certificate programs represent possible areas for further exploration. As resources continue to become more scarce, it has been suggested that there may be a new economic rationale for partnerships that focus on joint ventures. Without generous subsidies for continuing education programs, academic centers and MSOs may have major incentives to explore joint ventures. Hollister commented that higher education is under increased pressure to demonstrate its social benefits.   He also suggested that joint ventures with community-based organizations such as MSOs will be helpful to academic institutions as they "re-negotiate their social compact with society."

There is already evidence that successful collaborative programs are possible. In Philadelphia, La Salle University and the Nonprofit Management Development Center (NMDC) have developed a strong synergistic relationship. NMDC has been housed within the School of Business Administration since 1981.   In their paper, "Bridging the Scholar/Practitioner Gap," Kathryn Szabat and Karen Simmons, executive director of NMDC, describe the valuable relationship that has evolved between the two organizations. Consulting and training services, as well as research efforts, have all benefited from the relationship between La Salle and NMDC.   They conclude their paper with a note of optimism for future partnerships:

At La Salle NMDC, there is a history of the academic center working together with the MSO. None of the points noted in this paper were planned and designed; rather, they evolved out of an organic organizational growth process. We can continually grow together, as long as we continue to recognize the strengths of both practitioners and faculty. (Simmons and Szabat, 1996a, p. 4)

In Southern California, the Volunteer Center of Orange County coproduces two certificate programs in nonprofit management with the California State University at Long Beach and the University of California at Irvine. In Los Angeles, the National Society of Fund Raising Executives and UCLA codeveloped a successful certificate program on nonprofit management.

Another opportunity for joint venturing exists in the delivery of degree-based learning programs. MSOs can supplement the academic experience by offering rewarding internship placements to master's degree students. Life is messy, and students need exposure to the messiness. MSOs can provide students with opportunities to work with real organizations facing real problems that go beyond the neatly crafted case studies that are likely to be found in textbooks. In return for well-supervised internships, MSOs can expand their service capacity by undertaking projects staffed by students.

There is a wealth of evidence that such internships can serve the learning goals of students and the programmatic interests of MSOs. One example cited during the interviews involved the University of Rhode Island's psychology department evaluation and research team. University students were placed at the Support Center of Rhode Island to help develop evaluation models for the center's management training program. As part of the process, students worked with nonprofit clients, professional trainers, and Support Center staff, and faced practical real-life issues that a professional evaluator would be required to address in an actual evaluation project.

CONCLUSION

Discussions with MSO practitioners and academics produced substantial agreement on the benefits of seeking productive collaboration. There is already significant interest and support for such collaboration. Indeed, such partnerships are already occurring in a handful of isolated areas, and greater collaboration between the two fields seems inevitable. Clearly, stronger collegial relationships will have to precede quantum leaps in collaborative work. Real barriers, such as differing institutional cultures, vastly different professional pressure points and methodologies, limited financing, and too few common "meeting grounds" are threats to progress. However, as the need for and benefits of partnership between the academic centers and the management support profession become more apparent, existing obstacles will yield to the real potential of a strong strategic alliance.

APPENDIX 9.1
INTERVIEWS

Jane Arsenault, former Executive Director, Support Center of Rhode Island

Kathleen Fletcher, Consultant, San Anselmo, CA

Emanual Forster, Partner, Forester-Gilbert Associates, Los Angeles

Larry Guillot, Executive Director, Center for Management Assistance, Kansas City, MO

Hedy Helsell, Executive Director, The Center for Nonprofit Management, Dallas; President, Nonprofit Management Association

Robert Hollister, Dean, Graduate School of Arts and Sciences, Tufts University, Medford, MA

Joe Mixer, Independent consultant, Berkeley, CA; Chair, Research Committee, National Society of Fund Raising Executives

Patty Oertel, former Executive Director, Center for Nonprofit Management in Southern California, Los Angeles

Michael O'Neill, Director, Institute for Nonprofit Organization Management, University of San Francisco

Bob Orser, Consultant, Santa Rosa, CA

Peggy Outon, Associate of Ogden Museum of Southern Art, New Orleans

Kathy Szabat, Statistician and Market Researcher, La Salle University Nonprofit Management Development Center, Philadelphia

Michael Seltzer, Program Officer, Ford Foundation

Nora Silver, Executive Director, Volunteerism Project, San Francisco

Karen Simmons, Executive Director, Nonprofit Management Development Center, La Salle University, Philadelphia

John Palmer Smith, Director, Mandel Center for Nonprofit Organizations, Case Western Reserve University, Cleveland

Carol Stone, Executive Director, Volunteer Center of Orange County, Santa Ana, CA

Part 3

Theoretical Issues

10

Games Universities Play: An Analysis of the Institutional Contexts of Centers for Nonprofit Study

Dennis R. Young

INTRODUCTION

Over the past two decades, more than two dozen university centers devoted to the study of nonprofit organizations have been established at universities in the United States and around the world. These centers span a wide swath of scholarly and applied intellectual territory, including legal, public policy, social science, and international nonprofit sector studies. Several centers concentrate specifically on management of nonprofit organizations. The nonprofit centers also offer a variety of services, including graduate education and noncredit executive education for managers, trustees, and young scholars; technical assistance for nonprofit organizations; and research on various aspects of the nonprofit sector. Some centers concentrate primarily on one of these services while other centers maintain more comprehensive portfolios.

Centers of nonprofit study are organized in a variety of ways within their universities. Some are freestanding, but most are contained within a given school, college, institute, or department. A key question for the long-term development of nonprofit studies in universities is what kinds of internal arrangements will work best to ensure the long-term survival and development of these programs. Reynold Levy, Richard Cyert, Paul DiMaggio, Si Slavin, and Mark Keane and Astrid Merget each commented on aspects of this issue in the 1986 conference on "Educating Managers of Nonprofit Organizations" in San Francisco (O'Neill and Young, 1988, chapters 2, 3, 4, 6, and 10). Although their prescriptions varied, each of these scholars noted the difficulty of establishing and maintaining nonprofit programs within existing structures of the university. As Levy observed (p. 28), "Colleges and universities today too often treat nonprofits . . . interstitially, filling spaces in a curriculum dedicated to other purposes, driven by other needs. There is another, perhaps a better way."

Ten years later this essential truth still holds, but considerable experience has been gained by dozens of university nonprofit programs. Thus, the question of how best to organize such programs can now be revisited with greater confidence. The purpose of this chapter is to analyze this recent experience with an eye toward better understanding the issues that determine the long-term viability and prosperity of these centers. The approach is both conceptual and empirical.

First, the metaphor of games is offered as a conceptual framework for analyzing the organizational and decision-making contexts of nonprofit academic centers. Second, a survey of these centers provides descriptive detail on these units and the circumstances in which they operate. Third, six specific "games" involving centers and their various stakeholders are analyzed. Finally, implications of the game analysis for achieving the permanency and stability of these centers within their universities are explored.

The analysis makes clear that while nonprofit academic centers serve many important constituents and have garnered considerable support and acclaim, their fate still depends inordinately on a few powerful groups, including top officials in university administration and external funders. Thus, the long-term stability of the centers appears to hinge both on the mobilization of their primary beneficiaries and on the continued cultivation of powerful allies. Alternatively, structural changes may be needed to empower primary beneficiaries of the centers in order to overcome some of the disadvantages the centers face in playing the games under current rules. In that regard, however, Levy's caution appears to remain as true as ever: "The strong disciplinary orientation of the university is embodied in a potent departmental structure, jealous of its prerogatives, certain of its ground, wary of newcomers, and eager for any incremental resources. These forces militate strongly against enduring cooperative initiatives across disciplinary lines. They develop the strongest of antibodies when confronted with proposals for a novel, freestanding program" (O'Neill and Young, 1988, p. 29).

CONCEPTUAL FRAMEWORK

The metaphor of "games" is useful for analyzing the situations within which university nonprofit centers operate. There is ample precedent in the management, policy, and social science literatures for this approach to understanding behavior in complex institutional contexts. An early contribution by Norton Long (1958) described civic life in American communities as an "ecology" of separate, interactive games centered on local business, political, media, religious, and other social interests. Eric Berne's pioneering book (1964) discussed psychological games that people play with one another in their personal lives. Graham Allison's analysis (1971) of the Cuban missile crisis applies a bureaucratic politics game model as one of three paradigms to generate a full understanding of that conflict situation. Other examples include Susan Bernstein's analysis (1991) of the "game of contracted services" between government and nonprofit social service providers, Maital and Maital's characterizations (1984) of various economics games played at different levels of society, and McMillan's analysis (1992) of games faced by organizational managers. Game analysis has also been applied to such diverse circumstances as the Watergate scandal (Muzzio, 1982), Bible stories (Brams, 1980), and a variety of historical political situations and scenarios in classical literature (Brams, 1994).

Charles Monson (1967) wrote that universities have been described by dozens of different metaphors, ranging from zoos to egg-candling machines! Some of these metaphors, such as Clark Kerr's "city composed of anonymous citizens with diverse interests" (Monson, 1967, p. 22), suggest that game playing may be a useful way of understanding these institutions as well. The classic work of Michael Cohen and James March (1986, p. 3) on the university presidency also hints that universities, as "organized anarchies," are ripe for game analysis: "The American college or university is a prototypic organized anarchy. It does not know what it is doing. Its goals are either vague or in dispute. Its technology is familiar but not understood. Its major participants wander in and out of the organization. These factors do not make a university a bad organization or a disorganized one; but they do make it a problem to describe, understand, and lead."

The message here for nonprofit academic centers is decidedly mixed. These centers operate in a chaotic environment in which they must fend for themselves with modest resources. However, this environment is also one in which entrepreneurial initiative is important, in which sympathetic top university leadership can make a difference, and where skilled game players have a chance for success.

Robert Birnbaum's (1988) analysis of colleges and universities suggests even more strongly the utility of applying the framework of games to higher education. Birnbaum describes four complementary ways of understanding these institutions— as collegia, as bureaucracies, as political systems, and as organized anarchies. Each of these models incorporates aspects of games, but the political model is perhaps the most explicit: "To consider a college as a political system is to consider it as a supercoalition of subcoalitions with diverse interests, preferences and goals. Each of the subcoalitions is composed of interest groups that see at least some commonality of their goals and work together to attempt to achieve them" (p. 132).

Below, we will implicitly follow Allison's (1971) paradigm of the bureaucratic politics game, which utilizes the following organizing concepts:

- players in positions who can affect the decisions and outcomes of the situation;
- the stands taken by each player as determined by his or her perceptions and interests;
- the power and leverage each player brings to his or her position;
- the nature of the game itself, including the access each player has to particular means of influence, the rules of the game, and the manner in which the players interact with one another to produce a result.

University nonprofit centers operate within a layered context in which alternative players have different stakes and influences. The layers include the school or department in which a given center may be embedded, the university itself, the community where the university is located, and the national and international nonprofit and scholarly communities. The players include faculty, funders, university officials, students and alumni, and nonprofit sector constituents. The character of the games is likely to differ according to a given center's particular context, programmatic objectives, and structure, but all successful centers must negotiate games at several layers in order to ensure their viability and vitality. Indeed, centers may be viewed as participating in a series of simultaneous, interrelated games with different constituencies and concerning different aspects of their operations. They must attend to their success not only as academic units (teaching and research) but also as providers of information and consultation to local, national, and international constituents, as economic units that must make ends meet, and as conforming parts of their university bureaucracies and cultures. In all, the games in which these centers are enmeshed require that the centers' own needs be reconciled with those of the stakeholder groups with which they must do business.

SURVEY OF NONPROFIT ACADEMIC CENTERS

Directors of the 24 nonprofit centers belonging to the Nonprofit Academic Centers Council (NACC) in 1995 were surveyed by mail. Centers were asked about the size, scope, history, programming, organizational structure, and stakeholders in their organizations. Membership in NACC requires that a center be a formally organized unit within a university in the United States, with a director, a research component in its program, and a substantial explicit emphasis on the study of nonprofit organizations. In addition to NACC members, one center in the United Kingdom and one center in Canada, both meeting NACC criteria, were included in the survey. Responses were received from all 26 centers.

The median annual budget for reporting centers was between $100,000 and $500,000. Only two centers reported annual budgets of more than $3 million. Three of the six larger centers (over $1 million budget) were established in the 1970s or earlier, but two of these centers preexisted as more general policy or public service institutes that later took on nonprofit studies as a major emphasis.

The nonprofit centers are most commonly organized as separate units within an established school in the university. In most of these cases, the center director reports directly to a dean; in five cases, however, the center director reports to another director or an associate dean. Thirteen of the 26 centers are organized as integral units within schools. Another nine centers are freestanding within their universities, with the center director reporting to the president, the provost or other vice president, a dean, or a committee of deans. In four cases, the center is part of a larger department or institute, and the director reports to the chairperson or another director. The latter is more common among the smaller centers (under $100,000 budget). The freestanding arrangement is more common among the larger centers (four of six with budgets over $1 million) and among centers with budgets between $100,000 and $500,000 (four of eleven).

The survey asked center directors to prioritize their stakeholders in order of importance. Students, funders, faculty, alumni, university administration, nonprofit organizations in the local community or region, national nonprofit organizations, and international nonprofit organizations were listed as options, with a space for write-ins. Various respondents added "the academic community," "the nonprofit sector as a whole," "researchers," "users of knowledge," and "businesses, corporations, and government agencies" to the stakeholder list.

Within the top three priorities, the most frequently cited stakeholder group was students (18), followed by university administration (16), faculty (between 11 and 13, depending on interpretation of "researchers" and "academic community"), funders (10), community nonprofits (nine), and national nonprofits (six). Students were cited most frequently (nine times) as the highest priority stakeholder. While university administration was cited second most often among the top three stakeholders, it was most often listed as third priority (by eight centers). Similarly, while 13 centers cited faculty among the top three priorities, this group was also cited most commonly as a third priority (six centers). Perhaps surprisingly, funders were cited in the top three by only 10 centers, and these citations were spread fairly evenly among first, second, and third priority. No discernible differential pattern of priorities was found among centers of different sizes.

Clearly, a rich cast of characters is involved in nonprofit academic centers. As shown in Table 10.1, each key stakeholder group is reported to have specific demands on the centers and particular sources of influence over them. Students want a quality education, practical skills, and help with their careers; they influence centers primarily by voting with their tuition dollars. The university administration wants programs that enhance the prestige of the institution, bring in money, and are not costly or troublesome. This group generally has substantial control over the centers but can also be of enormous help to them. Tenure-track faculty look to the centers for research and teaching opportunities that will help them advance their careers; they hold sway over the centers through their willingness to participate and to confer academic legitimacy. Nonprofit organizations in the community, and indeed at the national and international levels as well, look to centers for information, educational programs, and help with their problems; they can influence the reputations of centers by ascribing relevance, utility, and quality to their activities and by offering opportunities for the centers to carry out their programs. Funders want high-quality programs to show for their investments, and they want services that will aid the work of nonprofit organizations in their fields of interest. They have the obvious leverage of funding over the centers. Alumni want continuing education and networking opportunities and assurance that centers will continue to enhance the credibility of their programs and credentials. Alumni have influence in their communities and can help the centers with resources and programming opportunities, support, and external funding.

Center directors were asked to identify the most crucial factors required to institutionalize their centers as permanent parts of their universities. Not surprisingly, directors of the smallest centers (under $100,000 annual budget) cited the need for expanded resources, including greater faculty and staff support, and external funding. They emphasized the need for help from university administration to secure staff and faculty support, to access external sources of funding, and to confer academic legitimacy to their programs. Respondents also noted the importance of achieving greater institutional understanding of their missions and academic legitimacy for the field of nonprofit studies.

The directors of centers with budgets between $100,000 and $500,000 echoed concerns over resources, including support for faculty and administrative positions, and internal and external funding. They cited needs for long-term institutional funding, administration support to seek outside funding, and building of endowments. This group also emphasized the importance of commitments by university administration and the board of trustees for recognizing the centers as viable, integral, and legitimate parts of the university. The importance of academic status, including recognition of the nonprofit arena in the graduate school curriculum, as a part of the student body, and as a legitimate field of research in tenure and promotion decisions, was also noted. Directors of these centers also identified marketing as an important need, including the development of linkages with learners, establishment of higher profiles for centers within their schools, and promotion of center programs to current and prospective students and faculty. They also identified increased faculty participation and center leadership that believes in the mission as important factors in achieving permanency.

Directors of centers with budgets of $500,000 to $1 million emphasized resource needs even more heavily, especially long-term sources of funds, including endowment funds for fellowships, scholarships, faculty chairs, and other uses, and funding for staff positions, faculty sabbaticals, and research. Respondents also noted the importance of developing and preserving earned income, including maintaining steady enrollments and tuition flows, and obtaining a fairer share of their generated income from university administration. Finally, these respondents cited public relations needs, including maintaining a good image and high productivity, and finding creative ways of involving faculty in the community.

Responses from the largest, more established centers (over $1 million budgets) reflect the perspective of organizations that have some sense of security but are nonetheless still concerned with achieving permanency. Respondents cited the need for stable financial support from endowments and hard money commitments from the university through core support for students, dedicated tenure track faculty, institutionalization of degree tracks, and access to library and building funds. A reciprocity was perceived between a university's commitment to the center's mission and delivering on the expectations of university administration, students, and faculty. In this spirit, the maintenance of the quality and visibility of the center's work and retaining a firm place within the university's culture and traditions were noted as important factors.

GAMES CENTERS PLAY

The influences and pressures identified by nonprofit academic center directors may be better appreciated by describing the games that centers must play with their various stakeholders. Six such games appear to be particularly important: the turf game, the priorities game, the control game, the faculty game, the funding game, and the community game.

The Turf Game

Nonprofit centers are carving out a new area of study within the university. Generally, the programs of the centers are interdisciplinary in character and hence impinge, at least potentially, on the academic territories of existing units. This constitutes both an opportunity and a problem for the centers. On the one hand, it allows the centers to build support by offering special research and teaching opportunities to faculty and graduate students in various parts of the university. On the other hand, the centers can be perceived as threats to other units, and they may have difficulty protecting their own territory when other units decide to start up nonprofit-related initiatives. As interdisciplinary initiatives in a new field of study, the centers

Table 10.1
Stakeholder Group Wants and Influences

Stakeholder	Wants From Center	Leverage
University administration	• Money (outside support) • University prestige, credit, recognition, respect, visibility • Student enrollments, tuition • Quality of programs, faculty, leadership in field • Good administration, low cost • Student employment • Model for university-community relations; community credibility and support • Leadership in public service research and education across university • Fundraising, public relations asset	• Budget and support services • Control over existence • Influence over internal legitimacy and reputation • Fundraising assistance • Approval of courses, program, appointments • Use of university name
Students	• Quality education, competent instruction, faculty attention • Employment assistance and opportunities for career advancement • Practical skills • Convenient arrangements • Networking • Credible, recognized credentials • Financial support • Help with student service organizations • Access to activities and resources of center and projects, intellectual stimulation	• Enrollment, participation • Tuition funds • Complaints to faculty • Influence over reputation in field, political influence, community public relations • Influence with university administration

Table 10.1 (cont'd.)

Faculty	
• Opportunities for research, teaching, and visibility • Funding support for research and innovative teaching • Academic career advancement • Quality academic programs, students, and materials • Contribution to school's rating in national polls • Support services and salary • Prestige and networking (adjuncts) • Training in community service learning • Developing relationships with nonprofit organizations • Role in program design and governance • Intellectual stimulation	• Participation and loss of interest • Influence over reputation and legitimacy • Power within school or university governance • Influence with university administration • Influence over program design • Influence in nonprofit community • Contribution to teaching
Community nonprofits	
• Information, materials, and dissemination of research • Professional and practice-oriented education and development opportunities • Technical assistance and advice • Forums for exchange of ideas; interesting programs • Qualified employees, trained students • Help with advocacy, public policy • Improved university-community relationships • Networking opportunities, national and international contacts	• Reputation and public relations, influence with funders and other stakeholders • Influence over enrollment • Validation of research relevance • Collaboration, sharing information • Program funding, purchasing reports • Influence with university administration • Referral of opportunities • Internships

National nonprofits	• Compilation and dissemination of research • Convening forums and networking opportunities • Executive and graduate level training/distance learning • Exposure and advocacy for nonprofit sector/public policy assistance • Advice and technical assistance • Participation in their networks	• Influence over reputation and legitimacy/public relations/visibility • Influence over enrollments • Participation in projects and information sharing • Validation of research relevance • Purchase of publications • Influence with funders • Referral of opportunities
Funders	• Credible programs, good products, completion of proposal objectives; quality work completed on time • Service to small nonprofits, helping nonprofits to manage better, improve stewardship of charitable gifts, build capacities • Sector leadership, impact on sector, public policy support • New, significant knowledge; dissemination of research findings • Neutral forum for convening sector representatives • Cutting-edge, high-quality, practice-oriented education	• Funding • Influence on legitimacy, existence • Ability to impose constraints
Alumni	• Networking opportunities • Employment information and assistance • Continuing education • Increased program prestige, reputation • Continued linkage to university	• Public relations, marketing help; ability to recruit students • Political, community influence, connections to nonprofits • Influence with faculty, university administration, and professional networks and reputation • Participation in center programs • Funding

Table 10.1 (cont'd.)

International nonprofits	• Information, advice, and technical assistance • Training and graduate education, distance learning • Participation in research projects, access to research results • Convening of conferences • Interaction with faculty • Brokering contacts with regional nonprofits and funders	• Enrollment • Participation in programs • Validation of research relevance • Collaboration, sharing of information • Purchase of publications • Public relations • Influence on reputation • Access to funders
Media	• Newsworthy activity • Source of commentary	• Reputation
Researchers	• Access to records • Funding assistance	• Publications and papers contributing to center's mission

do not have the same claims as traditional discipline-based departments or schools. The turf issue is mitigated for centers falling within a single traditional school such as public administration or business administration, where claims can be sorted out internally according to some plan. Even here, however, centers must compete for resources. Moreover, this arrangement leaves open the possibility that other schools in the university will develop parallel, if not competing, centers.

A particularly troublesome scenario develops when faculty with interests in non-profit studies receive support for their work from a nonprofit center outside their own school and then fail to acknowledge that support or decide to compete with it with independent initiatives of their own. Loyalty to an interdisciplinary center is a tenuous commodity that can be enforced with little more than appeal to conscience or promise of additional resources, unless faculty are somehow allowed to claim a degree of ownership or control in the center that competes with the pull of their home schools.

A long-term fear for centers is that they could be playing the role of market testers and that they will succeed in proving the legitimacy and viability of markets for nonprofit studies, only to have those markets taken over by traditional units within the university. Such a scenario may ultimately be healthy or unhealthy for the field. It may provide nonprofit studies with greater long-term stability, or it may risk their dilution and dissolution if the special sensitivity to nonprofit needs is lost in the process. In any case, the viability of nonprofit centers is threatened by this jockeying over turf.

The Priorities Game

Nonprofit centers often have difficulty gaining the attention they require within their universities in order to secure needed resources. At least three variations of the priority game are possible. First, a center may be located within a single school, where it must compete with other, more well-established programs in that school. Second, a center may be freestanding, in which case it must negotiate for its needs with established schools and faculties and must garner the support of central administration. Third, the center may itself be a collaboration of two or more established units (schools) of the university, in which case it must compete for the priorities within each collaborating school.

Each of these games is slightly different. Centers within existing schools have the problem of convincing colleagues in a relatively homogeneous disciplinary area that nonprofit studies is an important part of their field. This appears to be an easier case to make in some areas, such as public administration or social work, than in other areas, such as economics, law, or business administration. But in all cases, it requires changing traditional ways of thinking within the established discipline.

Focusing nonprofit studies within a single school also risks losing the contributions and creativity that can result from crossing disciplinary lines within the university. Nonetheless, a center within a single school probably has a better chance of getting its priorities taken seriously than does an alternatively organized center, because it competes within a relatively smaller unit and relates more directly to the interests of that unit. Much depends on whether the leader of that unit (the dean or institute director) or its senior faculty have any special interest or affinity for nonprofit work or ascribe academic legitimacy to it.

Self-standing, interdisciplinary centers have the advantage of being able to define their programs on their own terms, without overbearing pressure to conform to the interests of a particular school or discipline. Moreover, these centers can more easily draw together a critical mass of faculty interested in nonprofit studies, by coalescing these faculty across disciplines. However, such centers cannot command the priorities of the schools on which they draw, and they must operate purely on a quid pro quo basis in order to secure faculty participation and other needed resources from the schools. In addition, these centers may have difficulty garnering the support of university administration because they represent relatively small programs, generally without faculty of their own and with still uncertain potentials for bringing resources and prestige to the university. The interest and support of university administration in this arrangement is nonetheless crucial.

Centers that are formed as collaborations of two or more schools within the university suffer the same problems as centers within single schools. They must convince colleagues within each school that nonprofit studies is important within their respective disciplines and should be supported. However, this problem is made worse by the fact that none of the collaborating schools receives full credit for the center's accomplishments. Hence, the center becomes a kind of "commons" in which collaborating schools try simultaneously to minimize their investments and maximize their returns. This situation may be mitigated to a degree if the central administration of the university or other influential parties take a special interest in the center. However, the efficacy of outside stimulus in this case is moderated by the degree of ownership and autonomy assumed by the collaborating schools. In the case of a decentralized university with strong deans, outside influence is unlikely to be highly effective. Indeed, the control of such programs at the level of schools provides cover for the university administration to stay out of the picture.

The Control Game

Nonprofit centers pose special issues of control within the context of universities. At the level of schools and colleges, deans much prefer to have control over centers rather than share control with other schools. Moreover, they prefer to have centers organized at the school level rather than having independent centers created that may impinge on their turf and compete for resources within the university. Thus, interdisciplinary collaborations are difficult to begin with and succeed only where outside pressure and incentives, from funders for example, are brought to bear. And even when such collaborations are established, they suffer from neglect. The incentive for deans is to keep the collaboration under control and enjoy whatever benefits may come out of it, without contributing much to it.

Different control problems exist at the level of central administration. While the provost and president may seek to maintain authority over deans and directors, they also want to minimize the administrative complexity of their tasks. One way to do this is to keep their spans of control low and hence to keep the number of management centers under their jurisdictions to a minimum. Thus, the formation of independent or freestanding centers represents a very mixed blessing for top university officials. In general, they would much rather see such programs subsumed within traditional units of the university than take separate responsibility for them. Moreover, in the case of nonprofit centers, the stakes may not be perceived as high enough to warrant their becoming arenas of conflict with deans. Presumably, central administration can be counted upon to become independent champions of nonprofit programs only where there is very substantial outside pressure from funders or the nonprofit community to do so, or if there is an issue of keeping an existing school from becoming too powerful, or where top university leadership firmly believes that nonprofit studies is an area of future growth that would be inhibited by subsuming it within a traditional school or department.

Understanding the control game is critical if nonprofit study is ever to become a major academic field of its own within the university. If nonprofit studies are intrinsically interdisciplinary and essentially different from offerings of existing departments, then university administration will have to be convinced that the benefits of assuming an additional administrative burden and challenging the political interests of deans and their faculties outweigh the costs of doing so.

The Faculty Game

The faculty game concerns securing the services of faculty members to participate in center research, teaching, and service programs. Three categories of faculty are involved, and each is associated with particular problems for a center. Pre-tenure junior faculty can be the most energetic, talented, and reliable faculty resources involved in a nonprofit center, but members of this group are overwhelmingly concerned with achieving tenure. As a result, they cannot independently choose to participate in a center's program even if they have a strong personal interest in doing so. They must first be assured that their departmental elders approve of such participation relative to other duties or interests, and they must be confident that research or teaching in the nonprofit center will be evaluated as a positive contribution to their disciplines. In some cases, center interests and junior faculty interests align nicely, for example, when the center can open up a fresh new area of research where the faculty member can make a significant impact on his or her field. Often, such potential goes unrecognized, out of ignorance or resistance from discipline-based faculty.

Senior tenured faculty have more flexibility to participate in nonprofit center programs and may indeed constitute a core strength of a center. Outstanding tenured faculty members who are devoted to nonprofit work can be a center's most important asset. The risks for the center are manifold with this group, however. Some senior faculty may have become unproductive, and both they and their departments may be looking to the center to usefully employ them. This situation can work well for all parties; just as likely, however, it provides centers with faculty resources of questionable value. Another serious risk is that senior faculty can be prima donnas. They work for the center when and if they want to, but there is little to hold them for the long run or to ensure their reliability.

A third category of faculty are adjuncts, practitioners in the community or administrative staff within the university who have special expertise and enjoy teaching. This group presents distinct advantages to the nonprofit center and indeed probably constitutes the bulk of faculty for most nonprofit academic centers today. Such individuals often have valuable specialized knowledge and experience, and they cost much less than regular faculty. Moreover, they may be disengaged fairly easily if their performance is not adequate. Nonetheless, they have some disadvantages. Adjuncts may be less accessible to students because they do not work primarily on campus, their knowledge of literature or their teaching ability may be limited, they offer centers little help in nonteaching functions such as research, and they do not command the same respect as regular faculty within the university. Provosts or deans concerned with traditional academic standards may frown on heavy use of adjuncts, and students may feel cheated if they do not have access to faculty with a grounding in research.

The Funding Game

Given the difficulties of competing for attention and resources within the university context, nonprofit centers depend heavily on the support of outside funders. This is especially true of centers in private universities that are driven by tuitions and grants, but it applies to public universities as well. The funding game involves both university administration and external funders. Within the university, centers must often compete with other internal priorities for permission to approach donors. Depending on how the center is organized, this issue may occur at the school level, where center interests vie with other school programs for inclusion in proposals to particular funders, or at the university level, where centers may be queued behind other units for access to certain donors. Universities differ in the way they handle this issue. Universities with entrepreneurial presidents and development officers may create relatively freewheeling environments with a minimum of policing except where funders themselves object to receiving multiple proposals from different parts of the university. In universities with more controlling leaderships, the traffic-cop function of the development office may be more heavy-handed. In this case, nonprofit centers have a difficult time competing against larger interests within the university. In more freewheeling environments, nonprofit centers are better able to prove their potential through entrepreneurial initiative.

Within the funding community itself, several different subgames are played. The *start-up* subgame may be the best known and the most frustrating. In this subgame, funders promise to provide initial capital for the establishment of initiatives, contingent on plans for long-term funding from other sources. This can be viable for programs able to eventually generate their own income, such as graduate or executive education programs that garner tuitions or registration fees. Even here, however, students in nonprofit programs often require scholarship assistance that must be financed from tuitions, grant funds, or endowment. The game is even more problematic for research, community service, or other programs that necessarily require continuing subsidy. The start-up game requires centers to plan earned income programs that can ultimately offset the costs of desired, non-income-earning programs or to convince their university hosts that long-run net costs are worth assuming.

Funders also frequently require the demonstration of "buy-in" by the university as a whole or by the schools sponsoring the center. This can be called the *matching commitments* subgame. It is a game that is hard for a center to win. University administrations and sponsoring schools look for centers to fund themselves and indeed to provide financial and other benefits to the university, rather than to generate new liabilities. Much of the matching commitments subgame is played on paper, with the pricing out and "commitment" of resources that the university would be obligated to provide whether or not the new program is funded.

A third subgame played with the funding community is the *naming* subgame. This involves the conferral of recognition and status to donors in exchange for their gifts. The university usually sets the rules for how much money must be provided for recognition at various levels. Certain prices exist for named scholarships, professorships, library collections, buildings, or indeed whole centers or schools, although most things are ultimately negotiable. One implication of this subgame is the incentive to skew programs to become more saleable to donors. This is part of a general temptation to think opportunistically about donor interests rather than what makes overall sense for a center's mission. Potential donors may contribute enormously to creative thinking to guide a center's development, but there are also tremendous pressures to cater to donor preferences at the expense of a more comprehensive vision.

A particularly fascinating and potentially frustrating aspect of the naming subgame is the risk of limiting the center's opportunities by selling the name too cheaply. A scholarship or professorship named at too low a price will set a precedent for future such namings. And the conferral of a donor's name to a center as a whole will inevitably limit the incentives for other potential donors to provide major support. A named center becomes associated with the donor, and other funders assume that that donor has an obligation to provide the bulk of its support and sources for its growth. Moreover, a center named for one party cannot easily convince the named donor or other potential donors that naming credit should be shared for future projects, such as a new program or building. Donor sensitivities run high in this area and must be tended to carefully.

The Community Game

Another set of important subgames involve nonprofit centers in their local communities. As many nonprofit centers intrinsically define their programs in relation to strengthening local nonprofit organizations, they are expected to contribute to those institutions in a variety of ways, including technical assistance, training, and consultation. Often the expectation of such assistance is implicit in the support that centers receive from local funding organizations. One subgame is the *serve-me* subgame, in which local nonprofit organizations and funders manifest their expectations that the nonprofit center will do its part in the community. Another subgame is the *I'm special* subgame, in which particular segments of the nonprofit community require custom treatment because they see themselves as unique within the nonprofit sector. A third subgame is the *expert advisory* subgame, in which business and other community leaders provide consultation and support in the expectation that their advice will be followed. Finally, because nonprofit academic centers often view themselves as operating not only at the community level but also at the national or international levels, they encounter the tensions of the *local/global* subgame. Each of these subgames requires nonprofit centers to respond to sometimes conflicting community and academic demands.

The *serve-me* subgame derives from expectations incurred in the process of establishing a nonprofit academic center. Universities are under increasing pressures to be responsive to the needs of their local communities. Nonprofit centers are logical units to help serve this end. If funding for the center has come from local community sources, there is likely to be an implied bargain that the center will provide needed help to nonprofit organizations in the community. The problem for the center here is that expectations can be set too ambitiously, creating tensions between community service objectives and academic goals. With limited faculty, student, and staff resources, centers face difficult trade-offs between the provision of technical assistance and training and the achievement of research and teaching goals. Moreover, centers may not compete well with professional consultants and commercial trainers in this arena and may have great difficulty engaging faculty in community work. Faculty can do consultation work on their own; they look to centers more for the academic opportunities they can provide. The key to the serve-me subgame is for the center to develop particular versions of consultation and noncredit educational programming that are consistent with academic objectives and constraints and that open up new opportunities for faculty. The problem is that such programming may be viewed as insufficient, and perhaps too esoteric, by frustrated community leaders.

The *I'm special* subgame reflects the fact that the nonprofit sector is highly heterogeneous, which creates tensions for centers that are designed to address nonprofit organizations across the board. This tension exists in all facets of center work, including formal university coursework and research. However, it is most strongly felt in the realm of community service. Perhaps the most severe version of this subgame manifests itself in the arts community, which resists, more than most subsectors, being lumped into the nonprofit sector as a whole. This subgame requires centers to develop a multifaceted approach to keep such groups in their fold. First, the center must focus its programming on the truly common, generic issues that bind nonprofits together—such as fundraising, governance, and volunteer management. Second, the center must ensure that applications of methodology addressed to these issues are sufficiently illustrated with examples from areas that consider themselves "special." Third, the center must emphasize attracting audiences from a diverse cross-section of the nonprofit sector, with substantial representation from special subsectors. Fourth, the center may wish to entertain occasional separate programs for special subsectors at a level that accommodates these groups without creating new pressures for wholly independent programming.

The tensions associated with the *I'm special* subgame are not confined to the spreading of resource use within the center. They may also manifest themselves in the form of competitive pressures within the university. In particular, this subgame creates opportunities for other university programs to chip away at the constituent base of the nonprofit center by setting up specialized programs. Unless the university is committed to maintaining the integrity of the center by restraining such competition, the viability of the center can be seriously undermined.

The *expert advisory* subgame is played with high-level, influential advisors and funders of the center. Nonprofit centers require strong support from community leaders, including successful business executives, professionals, and heads of foundations and other major nonprofit institutions. Such individuals provide invaluable assistance, ideas, and resources. But as bright and energetic people, they are rarely without opinions on what the center should be doing and how it should do it. Whether or not their ideas are sensible or conform to the strategic direction of the center, the better part of valor is always to listen attentively and often to lean strongly toward finding ways to respond. Community leaders understand that they serve only in an advisory capacity, and they usually respect academic discretion. Nonetheless, it requires careful balancing to remain both selective and respectful of their ideas and to avoid ruffling important feathers.

Finally, the *local/global* subgame creates pressures on nonprofit centers both to emphasize community work and to avoid it. The players in this game include local community leadership and internal university interests. Internally, centers are under some pressure to steer clear of community service where such service would compete with the local markets of other established university programs. Thus, centers are advised not to compete for certain segments of the local student body or to seek funding or research involvement with certain local subsectors that might "belong" to other university programs. Since the world is a big oyster, these pressures push centers to look outward to the national and international professional and practitioner worlds for their sustenance, support, and service mandates. This set of pressures is reenforced by a desire for traditional recognition in the university, which comes most strongly from national or international media and professional attention.

Within the local community, of course, the pressures associated with the *local/global* subgame are a bit different. Members of the local community are less impressed with international or national level achievements. While they may bask in some of the glow, they are much more concerned with direct benefits to the community. An exception to this rule may come, however, in the form of community organizations that provide technical assistance to local nonprofits and may fear competition from university centers. Those organizations would just as well have the university centers operate primarily outside the local community.

These games and subgames constitute a complex field (some might say minefield!) of relationships that nonprofit academic centers must navigate in order to prosper. Many of the games illustrate the special problems associated with the peculiar character of centers in relation to conventional schools and departments within the university and the difficulty of overcoming entrenched interests and customs. Thus, center directors are faced with finding sources of leverage that will allow them to build their programs against the natural grain of the institution.

DISCUSSION

Four of the six principal games in which nonprofit centers are enmeshed—the turf, priorities, control, and faculty games—require these centers to deal directly, and on uneven terms, with powerful, largely indifferent, and sometimes antagonistic internal university interests, especially university administration, and deans and host faculties of various traditional schools and departments. This is true to an extent of the funding and community games, as well. It is these powerful but disinterested groups that centers must avoid antagonizing and to which they must appeal for support. In contrast, the groups and constituencies that benefit most from the centers and have the largest stake in their success are the least powerful and well organized and the least able to influence the outcomes of most of these games. As a result, center directors are also enmeshed in an overall "meta-game" that might be called the *latent group game* in deference to Mancur Olson's (1965) analysis of the problems large groups face in mobilizing themselves to promote their collective interests. Another way of saying this is that there is a general "audience" for the work of the nonprofit centers that has a genuine direct interest but is poorly organized to play in the primary university games (Long, 1958). In the meta-game, centers try to mobilize these latent interests as best they can to offset their weaknesses in the primary games.

The latent groups that have the greatest stakes in the nonprofit centers are students; alumni of center programs; diverse faculty with nonprofit sector interests, who are spread thinly throughout the university and in the practitioner world; various nonprofit organizations in the local, national, and global communities that benefit from center services; and the nonprofit academic research community at large. In addition, given the intrinsic tenuousness of this new academic field, directors of centers across the country have an important stake in each other's success. None of these groups is very powerful or easily mobilized, given their size, diversity, and geographical dispersion, nor is any of them directly connected into the decision-making apparatus of the universities, except in advisory capacities or as market segments. By contrast, the university presidents, provosts, deans, and host faculties have concentrated power and authority over the centers that can be effectively offset only by external funding, significant enrollments and tuitions, deft politicking, and a well-publicized record of success. This picture may change in years to come, as student and alumni groups grow larger and potentially more influential and as center directors align themselves with each other and build coalitions with funders and the nonprofit organizations they serve. Through more effective collective action by their currently weak and poorly organized latent interest groups, centers may ultimately succeed in strengthening their positions in the primary games they must play.

Alternatively, it may eventually be recognized that the difficulties of centers are essentially structural and can only be fully addressed by reorganizing them so that their key stakeholders (the latent groups) have requisite authority and leverage. In other words, change the rules of the games. This would mean transforming nonprofit academic centers into more traditional university structures, such as schools or colleges, and empowering students, alumni, faculty, nonprofit communities of interest, staff, and directors in the conventional ways that legitimize and normalize their authority and resources within the university setting. Given the extant games that must be played to achieve this state, such a transformation may be a long time in coming. Nonetheless, centers of nonprofit study have done reasonably well in playing the games to date, and a few have become modestly significant operations. Playing under the current rules, some may succeed in reaching a level that suggests essential parity with traditional units. At that juncture, transformation to a more conventional structure may be easier to achieve. In the words of a wise emeritus professor and university administrator, "If it looks like a school and smells like a school, it may eventually become a school." Until the rules change, however, center leaders must continue to amuse themselves and promote their causes by playing their multiple games against more challenging odds.

11

Nonprofit Management Education: A Field Whose Time Has Passed?

Lester M. Salamon

INTRODUCTION

In posing the question that forms the subtitle of this chapter, it is not my intention to reject the proposition that nonprofit organizations comprise a distinguishable sector with significant and distinctive management challenges. I have devoted too much of my life to studying this set of organizations to make that kind of case. Nor do I intend to question the immense contribution made by those who pioneered the development of separate nonprofit training programs—most notably Dennis Young and Michael O'Neill. Those contributions are what make it possible even to pose the issue I want to examine. But I am increasingly convinced that as a freestanding academic enterprise, nonprofit management education, for all its value and contributions, may represent the right answer to the wrong question. At the very least, it is by no means the *only* answer and is almost certainly not the *best* answer.

The three basic issues I will address in this chapter are: (1) What is the central question we should be facing in the field of nonprofit management education? (2) To what extent does nonprofit management education as currently practiced contribute to an effective response? (3) Finally, what could and should be done to respond to this question more effectively?

WHAT IS THE CENTRAL QUESTION?

To determine whether nonprofit management education as currently practiced is an appropriate answer, we naturally have to begin with the question to which it is the response. For those involved in the development of nonprofit education, that question has been fairly straightforward. As O'Neill and Young (1988, p. 1) put it in their excellent conference volume on the topic, the central issue to be addressed is, "How [should] managers of [private nonprofit organizations] be educated or trained"?

While this is obviously an intelligent and logical starting point for the design of a new training program in this world of customer-driven education, I am persuaded that there is a prior question that needs to be asked and that may lead us down a somewhat different road. That question is: *What is the central challenge, particularly the central management challenge, confronting efforts to solve our most pressing societal problems?*

This question assumes that nonprofit organizations serve important public purposes related to the solution of societal problems and not simply private purposes related to the interests of the organizations and their members and staff. While this is not an unrebuttable assumption, it seems a reasonable one for institutions that have objectives other than generating profits and consequently receive tax and other benefits from the public. Even those nonprofit agencies that seldom engage in policy debate are public-serving to the extent that their activity addresses public problems. Therefore, those concerned about improving the operation of the nonprofit sector cannot focus solely on the internal needs of these organizations; they must focus as well on the broader societal purposes these organizations are intended to serve and for which they must consequently be equipped.

The Central Challenge

What, then, is the central management challenge facing public problem-solving, and what implications does this have for the design of nonprofit management education? The answer to this question is not the challenge of improving general nonprofit management. Rather, the central challenge confronting efforts to solve public problems is the challenge of learning how to manage the complex collaborative relationships among the sectors that now form the heart of public problem-solving in virtually every sphere, both in the United States and, increasingly, around the world.

Such collaborations have long been an important feature of the American approach to public problems. This is how we built our railroads and canals, fought our wars, established our colleges, built many of our cultural institutions, revolutionized our agriculture, and dealt with the influx of immigrants into our cities. The nineteenth century saw extensive collaboration between local governments and private nonprofit groups. As of 1898, for example, 60 percent of the funds the City of New York spent on the care of paupers and prisoners went to private benevolent institutions. Similar practices were evident in all but four American states (Fetter, 1901/02, pp. 360, 376).

While such collaborations have long characterized the American approach to public problems, they have grown massively in scope and scale in recent decades. Health, education, housing, community development, day care, nursing home care, drug treatment, employment and training, and even arts and culture exhibit a complicated mixture of public and private action, not simply operating side by side but intimately intertwined. The "marble cake" metaphor that political scientist Morton Grodzins (1966) conjured up to describe the interplay of federal, state, and local government roles in the operation of American federalism and that he posited as an alternative to the inaccurate "layer cake" imagery embodied in the legalistic doctrine of "dual federalism" now applies more generally to the relations not only among levels of government but also among the different sectors. As former Independent

Sector president Brian O'Connell once put it, we are increasingly making a "mesh" of things in field after field of public action, combining public and private action in ever more imaginative and complicated ways. The result is an elaborate pattern of what I have elsewhere called "third-party government," of reliance by government on a host of "third parties" to carry out public programs and the extensive sharing by these third parties of important elements of discretionary authority over public efforts (Salamon, 1981, 1989). Indeed, in the United States "third-party government" has become the dominant pattern of government action in the domestic sphere, and it increasingly dominates the design of policy in other countries as well (Gidron, Kramer, and Salamon, 1992; Salamon and Anheier, 1998).

The forms as well as the scale of this collaboration are expanding greatly. Traditional purchase-of-service contracts now take their place among a dizzying array of other policy instruments through which governmental authority is shared with a wide variety of third-party institutions. These include grants, cooperative agreements, tax subsidies, vouchers, reimbursement systems, franchises, loans, loan guarantees, insurance, regulation, and many more. Each of these distinct "tools of public action" has its own, often complicated, operating procedures, its own skill requirements, its own characteristic delivery system, and hence its own implications for the likely outcome of public efforts (Salamon, 1981, 1989; Kettl, 1988). Each therefore has its own management demands both for those in the public sector and for those managing its partner institutions.

Nor does this trend seem likely to abate. To the contrary, "third-party government," once viewed as at best a necessary evil to get around America's congenital hostility to bureaucracy while responding to the need for expanded governmental services, is now being embraced as a positive virtue in the current widespread campaign to "reinvent government" (Osborne and Gaebler, 1992). According to this perspective, the problem with American government is that it is not sufficiently "entrepreneurial." What is needed, therefore, is

- to promote *competition* among service providers;
- to *empower* citizens by pushing control out of the bureaucracy and into the community;
- to redefine clients as customers and offer them choices;
- to rely on *market mechanisms* rather than bureaucratic mechanisms;
- to *catalyze* other sectors rather than simply providing services;
- in a word, to "steer" rather than "row." (Osborne and Gaebler, 1992, pp. 19–20)

In short, what is needed is a further, more radical dose of third-party government.

While third-party government or "entrepreneurial government" may ultimately improve the way we meet public needs, it is not without its own management challenges. To the contrary, for all its attractions, this pattern of government action poses immense management difficulties. Each of the many tools of government action represents a complex system with its own dynamics, procedures, and rules. With authority dispersed between government and nongovernmental actors, it is often difficult to fix responsibility or sort out respective roles. Managing these extended chains of indirection thus requires skills that go well beyond the management of either a public or a private agency. Managers on both sides of the institutional divide must understand the dynamics of their counterpart institutions as well as the particular requirements of the tool of public action through which they are inter-twined. Both public managers and the managers of third-party institutions must come to understand how to function across the borders of their respective organiza-tions, how to manage not public or private institutions but the *complex collaborative systems* linking the two.

The central challenge, particularly the central management challenge, confronting efforts to solve our pressing societal problems is *to prepare people to design and manage these immensely complex collaborations and networks that we increasingly rely on to address our public problems.*

Implications for Nonprofit Organizations

These developments naturally have significant implications for for-profit as well as nonprofit organizations. For-profit firms are actively engaged with government in building military equipment, extending guaranteed credit, providing home health services, and performing dozens of other tasks. Nevertheless, the implications for nonprofits are particularly striking. For better or for worse, nonprofit organizations have been particularly involved in this widespread expansion of America's system of third-party government, and for good reason. Nonprofit organizations often lead the way in responding to public problems and then mobilize support to enlist govern-ment aid. With established capabilities in a field and significant political support, they are therefore often in a position not only to assist in the operation of public programs but also to insist on a meaningful role in whatever public action results.

It is no accident that the period of most rapid expansion of government domestic activity in the United States was also the period of most dramatic growth of the na-tion's private nonprofit sector. Instead of the inherent antagonists sometimes pic-tured in conservative rhetoric, government and nonprofit organizations are more nearly natural allies, sharing a common commitment to solving public problems and, through the instruments of third-party government, finding a mechanism to join forces in pursuit of this goal. As a consequence, government-nonprofit cooperation has long been a characteristic feature of American life (see, for example, Bremner, 1980; Whitehead, 1973; Nielsen, 1979) and has emerged in recent years as the prin-cipal feature of the nation's human service delivery system. As just one reflection of this, a larger share of *government-funded* human services is delivered by *nonprofit* providers in the United States than is delivered by federal, state, and local govern-ments combined; and government support now outdistances private support to non-profit organizations by a factor of nearly two to one (Salamon, 1995).

With the new stress on "social capital" and civic renewal that has recently come to animate national policy debate, this focus on partnership and collaboration seems likely to grow. Indeed, nonprofit organizations are increasingly being viewed not simply as service providers but as community-builders and sector-spanners fostering cooperation with business and government to cope with public problems and im-prove the quality of community life. As a consequence, even those types of non-profits least engaged in formal cooperative ties with government to deliver public services (for example, religious organizations, advocacy organizations, arts organi-zations) are still likely to be enmeshed in complex collaborative relationships that span sector lines.

My argument is this: If the management of the complex collaborative systems linking government and a host of third-party partners has become the central management challenge confronting our efforts to cope with public problems and improve community life, then this challenge has special implications for the training of non-profit managers because of the central role that nonprofit organizations have come to play in this elaborate third-party system.

HOW IS THIS QUESTION BEING ADDRESSED?

To what extent is this challenge being addressed in the way we are preparing those who will operate these collaborative systems? And what, in particular, has the invention of nonprofit management education contributed to this process? Although I have not had a chance to review current course offerings at any of the three major types of training programs relevant to this question (public administration, public policy, and nonprofit management), my overall impression is that the answer to this question to date must still be, "Not much." At the very least, it is certainly, "Not nearly enough."

Public Administration

The most likely venues for training the border managers for our vastly expanded systems of third-party government are schools of public administration. Regrettably, however, public administration has been slow to pick up on this new reality. The central unit of analysis in public administration continues to be the public agency. The principal task of public administration training has consequently been to equip students with an understanding of the internal characteristics and operating features of public agencies: how they secure and manage personnel, how they secure and manage funds, and how they execute their tasks.

Although public administration has significantly shaken off its old orthodoxy about the separation between policy and administration and recognized the political dimensions of agency management, both externally and internally, notions of hierarchy and a preoccupation with internal agency operations still dominate the field (Ostrom, 1989; Seidman, 1986). Still largely ignored are the extent to which the public administration problem has leapt beyond the borders of the public agency, the multiple instruments through which public action now proceeds, the distinctive management challenges that these different instruments entail, and the multiple nongovernmental or other-governmental institutions that are consequently involved in the implementation of public programs.

Although a considerable number of public administration programs have recently added courses on the nonprofit sector to the ones they offer on public agencies, these emerged rather late in the process. What is more, these courses apply the same agency focus to a different type of organization rather than incorporating any significant reconceptualization of the nature of public administration.

Public Policy

The record of the newer schools of public policy in this matter is not much more heartening. The field of public policy emerged not out of concern about the inadequacies of *management* training for the public sector but out of concern about the failure to apply sophisticated economic and statistical analysis to the comprehension and solution of public problems. Although the new field of policy studies was taking shape and beginning its struggle for academic legitimacy during precisely the period when the system of third-party government was experiencing its most explosive growth, the 1960s and 1970s, public policy studies largely ignored the implementation side of the policy process or gave it very short shrift. Not until the mid 1970s was this "missing link" (Hargrove, 1975) even acknowledged in a serious way. Indeed, given the limited cachet that management enjoyed in the academic world at the time, at least outside business schools, the entrepreneurs of the new discipline of policy sciences understandably led with the more empirical parts of their new discipline—microeconomics, statistics, decision trees, mathematical simulations, evaluation studies, and the like—giving the field a technocratic caste that it has still not really shaken. In the process, little explicit attention was given to the distinctive management challenges posed by the numerous new instruments of policy action coming into widespread use. The one possible exception was the attention lavished on the policy instrument of *regulation*. But even here the focus was less on the management of regulatory programs than on the formulation of economic alternatives to them. Schools of public policy gave little or no attention to the challenge of training the border managers for the increasingly complex systems of public and private action or equipping these managers with an under-standing of how public and private agencies interact.

NONPROFIT MANAGEMENT

It was against this backdrop that the new and separate field of nonprofit management education took shape. At least part of the motivation for the form that this development took, understandably enough, was the conviction that "what's sauce for the goose should be sauce for the gander." If the two other sectors, government and business, deserved their own management schools or programs, then the nonprofit sector did, too. After all, this sector was also sizable and had its own distinctive qualities, such as the ambiguity of its performance criteria, the legal and financial constraints under which it operates, the sources of some of its financial support, the kinds of personnel it employs, and the governance structures of its organizations (O'Neill and Young, 1988, p. 3). It therefore faced its own distinctive management challenges. Specialized programs of nonprofit management were created at places like the University of Missouri at Kansas City, Case Western Reserve University, the University of San Francisco, and Indiana University.

Let me be clear: I am not criticizing this development. At the time, it made a great deal of sense. It represents what we might term the "Rodney Dangerfield solution" to the nonprofit sector's long-standing problem. Unable to get any real respect in the existing bastions of management training dominated by business and government, those interested in nonprofit management understandably struck out on their own—and with good effect. By attracting resources and students, they have established a force to be reckoned with and demonstrated the existence of a market for their product. Indeed, much of the newfound interest in the nonprofit sector among public administration schools can be traced to the successful competition that these nonprofit management programs posed to them.

But the nonprofit management education programs have not yet fashioned a suitable response to the central management challenge confronting efforts to solve public problems. Indeed, the establishment of separate programs of nonprofit management may have moved us in the opposite direction by splitting the training of nonprofit managers off from the training of the public managers with whom they will increasingly interact and forcing by students interested in public problems to choose between government and nonprofit careers, although many graduates' careers will take them into both sectors. In so doing, it violates one of the central principles that early advocates of nonprofit management education emphasized, that "the focus for nonprofit management education should be on careers, not specific organizations or types of organizations" (O'Neill and Young, 1988, p. 17). It also reinforces the misleading myths of voluntarism and splendid isolation that have kept us from understanding the true position of the nonprofit sector in modern society.

To put it in Hegelian terms, the establishment of specialized nonprofit management education programs has usefully posed a counterweight, an antithesis, to the preexisting programs of public administration and business management. The most important consequence of this is that it may have set the stage for a new synthesis that might provide a better response to the central challenge we face.

WHAT SHOULD BE DONE?

What might this new synthesis look like? How should we respond to the central management challenge we face in responding to public problems? Clearly, there is no one answer to this question any more than there is one answer to the question of how to train nonprofit managers. But the program we have fashioned at Johns Hopkins University certainly represents one possible response.

Focus on the Career: The Professional Citizen

At the heart of our program is a form of training that takes as its central unit of analysis not a particular type of organization but a particular type of career. That career is the career of the professional citizen.

A professional citizen is a person who is trained to work on public problems—to identify them, analyze them, devise solutions to them, and implement actions that alleviate them—whether the person works in governmental agencies, nonprofit organizations, or even for-profit companies in roles that focus on the solution of public problems, such as corporate philanthropy programs. A professional citizen is therefore not simply a public servant but a person who is professionally equipped to deal with public problems from any of a number of possible institutional vantage points.

Training Professional Citizens

What type of training does the career of professional citizen require? As we have conceived it at Johns Hopkins, it involves at least four crucial features, as follows.

First, we train nonprofit and public managers together, not apart. This reflects our realization that these two sets of institutions are increasingly intertwined in actual operation and are likely to become more so over time, that aspiring professional citizens often do not know whether they are likely to end up in government or nonprofit institutions and in fact often spend significant amounts of time in both, and that these two sets of institutions share common objectives and are therefore likely to attract similar types of personnel, who have the same ethos and speak the same language. By contrast, locating nonprofit training programs within business schools on grounds that "management is management" seems a far less persuasive proposition.

Second, we believe the training of professional citizens should emphasize the moral and philosophical underpinnings of public service and not simply the analytical or managerial requirements. We do this in our program by focusing on the concept of citizenship. Citizenship defines the essential set of rights and responsibilities that individuals enjoy as part of a community, and the corresponding rights and responsibilities that communities enjoy vis-à-vis individuals. The concept of citizenship combines notions of *justice* with concepts of *community* (Kymlicka and Norman, 1994, p. 352). As such, it defines the appropriate domain of public or collective action, providing the conceptual glue that ties the different branches of public service together and also providing the moral compass for the professional citizen, whether operating in the nonprofit or the public sector. As the British social theorist T.H. Marshall (1965, p. 92) put it,

Citizenship is a status bestowed on those who are full members of a community. All who possess the status are equal with respect to the rights and duties endowed. There is no universal principle that determines what those rights and duties shall be, but societies in which citizenship is a developing institution create an image of an ideal citizenship against which achievement can be measured and towards which aspiration can be directed.

Debating the image of that "ideal citizenship"—and it is a debate—must therefore be a central part of the training of a professional citizen.

Third, the training of professional citizens should include detailed exposure to the tools of government action, to the distinctive forms of the collaborative systems through which the public's business is increasingly done. As we have seen, these tools of action are numerous and varied. What is more, they involve different management tasks and enlist different sets of institutions. Persons who will serve as the border managers of these collaborations therefore need to have an intimate knowledge not only of the internal dynamics of the different types of institutions engaged in the collaborations but also of the distinctive management tasks and the peculiar pathologies to which each "tool" is prone. Instead of experts simply on different institutions, we therefore also need experts on the different tools through which these institutions interact.

Finally, the training of professional citizens also needs to encompass the basic rudiments of *management and policy analysis*, such as how to assess the scope and character of complex public problems, how to evaluate the impact of interventions, and how to develop and implement strategic plans.

The type of training I am describing is certainly no panacea. It is not a substitute for mid-career training for persons who have already chosen careers in the nonprofit sector. What is more, key elements of this package could be integrated into existing nonprofit and public policy curricula. But, as a model for responding to the central management challenge confronting our efforts to solve complex public problems, this model has much to recommend it. Instead of beginning with an assumption of sectoral independence, comforting though that might be, it acknowledges from the outset the fundamental interdependence of social sectors and prepares managers to deal explicitly with this reality. It thus trains managers in both public and private agencies to manage the complex systems that increasingly characterize our approaches to public problems. Beyond this, it provides a better fit with the career paths that professional citizens are increasingly likely to pursue.

CONCLUSION

Lord Nathan, the chairman of a postwar commission on the voluntary sector in the United Kingdom, pointed out some 50 years ago that "while a society is alive and growing it will not make rigid choices between state action and voluntary action, but both alike will expand as the common expression of its vitality" (quoted in Owen, 1964, p. 523). Americans have taken this dictum to heart in the design of our public programs, blending public and nonprofit action in immensely inventive ways. What we have yet to do, however, is take it to heart in the design of our governmental and nonprofit training. The great contribution of nonprofit management education programs as a counterpoise to the preexisting public administration and business management programs may well be that, by elevating the nonprofit side of the equation, it has at last set the stage for a new synthesis, for a truly new form of combined public service training. This, at any rate, is the real management and training challenge we face. And it is therefore the challenge we have designed our own program to address.

References

Allison, G.T. 1971. *The Essence of Decision.* Boston: Little, Brown and Company.

Argyris, C., and D. Schon. 1978. *Organizational Learning: A Theory-in-Action Perspective.* Reading, MA: Addison-Wesley.

Association for Volunteer Administration. 1995. *Welcome to the Future of Volunteer Leadership.* Boulder, CO: Association for Volunteer Administration.

Auld, C. 1995. *Professionalisation of Australian Sport Administration: The Effects on Organisational Decision Making. A Report to the Australian Sports Commission.* Brisbane: Griffith University.

Avis, R.K., and A.D. Trice. 1991. "The Influence of Major and Internship on the Evaluation of Undergraduate Women's Resumes." *College Student Journal* 25:536–538.

Batsleer, J. 1995. "Management and Organisation." In J.D. Smith et al. (eds.), *An Introduction to the Voluntary Sector.* London: Routledge.

Batsleer, J., C. Cornforth, and R. Paton. 1991. *Issues in Voluntary and Nonprofit Management.* Wokingham, England: Addison-Wesley.

Berne, E. 1964. *Games People Play.* New York: Ballantine Books.

Bernstein, S.R. 1991. *Managing Contracted Services in the Nonprofit Agency.* Philadelphia: Temple University Press.

Billis, D. 1993. *Organising Public and Voluntary Agencies.* London: Routledge.

Billis, D., and M. Harris (eds.). 1996. *Voluntary Agencies: Challenges of Organisation and Management.* London: Macmillan.

Birnbaum, R. 1988. *How Colleges Work.* San Francisco: Jossey-Bass.

Bowen, W.G., and W.J. Baumol. 1968. *Performing Arts: The Economic Dilemma.* Cambridge: MIT Press.

Brams, S.J. 1980. *Biblical Games.* Cambridge: MIT Press.

Brams, S.J. 1994. *Theory of Moves.* New York: Cambridge University Press.

Bremner, R. 1980. *The Public Good: Philanthropy and Welfare in the Civil War Era.* New York: Alfred A. Knopf.

Bruce, C.E. 1993. "Companies Prefer Hiring College Graduates with Experiential Education." *Black Collegian* 24:76–81.

Brudney, J.L. 1990. *Fostering Volunteer Programs in the Public Sector: Planning, Initiating, and Managing Voluntary Activities.* San Francisco: Jossey-Bass.

Brudney, J.L. 1992. "Administrators of Volunteer Services: Their Needs for Training and Research." *Nonprofit Management and Leadership* 2 (3):271–282.

Brudney, J.L., and T.M. Kluesner. 1992. "Researchers and Practitioners in Nonprofit Organization and Voluntary Action: Applying Research to Practice?" *Nonprofit and Voluntary Sector Quarterly* 21 (3):293–308.

Burt, G. 1994. "Management Development through Distance Learning: The Case of 'Managing Voluntary and Nonprofit Enterprises.' " Institute of Educational Technology, Open University, Milton Keynes, England.

Butler, P., and N. Collins. 1995. "Marketing Public Sector Services: Concepts and Characteristics." *Journal of Marketing Management* 11:83–96.

Carnegie Foundation for the Advancement of Teaching. 1977. *Missions of the College Curriculum: A Contemporary Review with Suggestions.* San Francisco: Jossey-Bass.

Chieco, K., D.S. Koch, and K.L. Scotchmer. 1996. *Mission Possible: 200 Ways to Strengthen the Nonprofit Sector's Infrastructure.* Washington, DC: Union Institute.

Clancy, P. 1995. *Managing the Cultural Sector: Essential Competencies for Managers in the Arts, Culture and Heritage in Ireland.* Dublin, Ireland: Oak Tree Press.

Cohen, M.D., and J.G. March. 1986. *Leadership and Ambiguity.* 2nd ed. Boston: Harvard Business School Press.

Crowder, N.L., and V.A. Hodgkinson. 1991. *Academic Centers and Programs Focusing on the Study of Philanthropy, Voluntarism, and Not-for-Profit Activity: A Progress Report.* 2nd ed. Washington, DC: Independent Sector.

Cyert, R.M. 1988. "The Place of Nonprofit Management Programs in Higher Education." In M. O'Neill and D.R. Young (eds.), *Educating Managers of Nonprofit Organizations.* New York: Praeger.

Den Hartog, D.N., J.J. Van Muijen, and P. Koopman. 1997. "Transactional versus Transformational Leadership." *Journal of Occupational and Organizational Psychology* 70 (1):19–34.

Department of Employment, Education and Training. 1995. *1994 Higher Education Student Data Collection.* Report 14. Canberra, Australia: The Department.

Department of Social Welfare. 1997. *Supporting Voluntary Activity: A Green Paper on the Community and Voluntary Sector and Its Relationship with the State.* Dublin, Ireland: Stationery Office.

DiMaggio, P.C. 1988. "Nonprofit Managers in Different Fields of Service: Managerial Tasks and Management Training." In M. O'Neill and D.R. Young (eds.), *Educating Managers of Nonprofit Organizations.* New York: Praeger.

Dinmore, I. 1997. "Interdisciplinarity and Integrative Learning: An Imperative for Adult Education." *Education* 117 (3):452–467.

Drucker, P.F. 1989. "What Business Can Learn from Nonprofits." *Harvard Business Review* (July–August) 89 (4):88–93.

Drucker, P.F. 1990. *Managing the Non-Profit Organization: Practices and Principles.* New York: HarperCollins.

Dudley, J.S., and J.S. Permaul. 1984. "Participation in and Benefits from Experiential Education." *Educational Record* 65:18–21.

Ellis, Susan. 1997. Interview by Gretchen E. Stringer with Susan Ellis, President of Energize, Philadelphia. August 7.

Faughnan, P., and P. Kelleher. 1993. *The Voluntary Sector and the State: A Study of Organizations in One Region.* Dublin, Ireland: Conference of Major Religious Superiors.

Fetter, F. 1901/1902. "The Subsidizing of Private Charities." *American Journal of Sociology* 7:359–385.

Fiedler, F.E. 1996. "Research on Leadership Selection and Training: One View of the Future." *Administrative Science Quarterly* 41(2):241–250.

Fisher, J.C., and K.M. Cole. 1993. *Leadership and Management of Volunteer Programs: A Guide for Volunteer Administrators.* San Francisco: Jossey-Bass.

Fishman, J.J., and S. Schwarz. 1995. *Nonprofit Organizations: Statutes, Regulations and Forms.* Westbury, NY: Foundation Press.

Gaff, J.G. 1991. *New Life for the College Curriculum: Assessing Achievements and Furthering Progress in the Reform of General Education.* San Francisco: Jossey-Bass.

Gaskin, K., and J. Davis Smith. 1995. *A New Civic Europe? A Study of the Extent and Role of Volunteering.* London: Volunteer Center U.K.

Gassler, S. 1990. "Nonprofit and Voluntary Sector Economics: A Critical Survey." *Nonprofit and Voluntary Sector Quarterly* 19 (2):137–149.

Gidron, B., R. Kramer, and L.M. Salamon. 1992. *Government and the Third Sector in Comparative Perspective: Experience in Modern Welfare States.* San Francisco: Jossey-Bass.

Goldstein, H. 1989. "Myths and Realities, Rewards and Frustrations of Working in the Nonprofit Sector." In L. Cohen and D. R. Young (eds.), *Careers for Dreamers and Doers.* New York: Foundation Center.

Greene, S.G. 1993. "Technology: Are Charities Missing the Revolution?" *Chronicle of Philanthropy* 6 (1):1, 26–31.

Grodzins, M. 1966. *The American System: A New View of Government in the United States.* Chicago: Rand McNally.

Grønbjerg, K.A. 1993. *Understanding Nonprofit Funding: Managing Revenues in Social Services and Community Development Organizations.* San Francisco: Jossey-Bass.

Gummer, B. 1996. "Total Quality Management: Organizational Transformation or Passing Fancy?" *Administration in Social Work* 20 (3):75–85.

Haas, P.J., and M.G. Robinson. 1996. "Square Pegs and Round Holes: The Views of Nonprofit Executives on Educating Nonprofit Managers." Presented at the Association for Research on Nonprofit Organizations and Voluntary Action conference, New York City.

Hackman, J.R., and R. Wageman. 1995. "Total Quality Management: Empirical, Conceptual and Practical Issues." *Administrative Science Quarterly* 40 (2):309–342.

Hall, P.D. 1994. "Historical Perspectives on Nonprofit Organizations." In R.D. Herman and Associates, *The Jossey-Bass Handbook of Nonprofit Leadership and Management.* San Francisco: Jossey-Bass.

Handy, C. 1981. *Understanding Voluntary Organisations.* Harmondsworth, England: Penguin.

Hargrove, E. 1975. *The Missing Link.* Washington, DC: Urban Institute.

Harridan, R. 1991. "The Liberal Matrix: Pluralism and Professionalism in the American University." *Journal of Higher Education* 62:451–466.

Harris, M. 1991. *Training and Education for the Voluntary Sector: The Needs and the Problems*. Working Paper 9. London: Center for Voluntary Organisations, London School of Economics.

Herman, R.D., and R.D. Heimovics. 1990. "The Effective Nonprofit Executive: Leader of the Board." *Nonprofit Management and Leadership* 1 (2):167–180.

Herman, R.D., and R.D. Heimovics. 1991. *Executive Leadership in Nonprofit Organizations: New Strategies for Shaping Executive-Board Dynamics*. San Francisco: Jossey-Bass.

Herman, R.D., and R.D. Heimovics. 1994. "A Cross-National Study of a Method for Researching Nonprofit Organizational Effectiveness." *Voluntas* 5 (1):86–100.

Hodgkin, C. 1993. "Rejecting the Lure of the Corporate Model." *Nonprofit Management and Leadership* 3 (4):415–428.

Hodgkinson, V.A. 1988. *Academic Centers and Programs Focusing on the Study of Philanthropy, Voluntarism, and Not-for-Profit Activity: A Progress Report*. Washington, DC: Independent Sector.

Hodgkinson, V.A., M.S. Weitzman, J.A. Abrahams, E.A. Crutchfield, and D.R. Stevenson. 1996. *Nonprofit Almanac, 1996–1997: Dimensions of the Independent Sector*. San Francisco: Jossey-Bass.

Hoefer, R. 1993a. "A Matter of Degree: Job Skills for Human Service Administrators." *Administration in Social Work* 17 (3):1–20.

Hoefer, R. 1993b. "Public Administration Educators and Nonprofit Human Services Administrators: Views on Desirable Skills and Degrees." *New England Journal of Human Services* 12 (3):4–12.

Home Office. 1989. *Charities: A Framework for the Future*. Cm 694. London, England: HMSO.

Home Office. 1990. *Profiting from Partnership: Efficiency Scrutiny of Government Funding of the Voluntary Sector*. London, England: HMSO.

Ilsley, P.J. 1990. *Enhancing the Volunteer Experience: New Insights on Strengthening Volunteer Participation, Learning, and Commitment*. San Francisco: Jossey-Bass.

Industry Task Force on Leadership and Management Skills. 1995. *Enterprising Nation: Renewing Australia's Managers to Meet the Challenges of the Asia-Pacific Century*. Canberra: Australian Government Publishing Service.

Kanter, R.M., and D.V. Summers. 1987. "Doing Well While Doing Good: Dilemmas of Performance Measurement in Nonprofit Organizations and the Need for a Multiple-Constituency Approach." In W.W. Powell (ed.), *The Nonprofit Sector: A Research Handbook*. New Haven: Yale University Press.

Keane, M.E., and A.E. Merget. 1988. "Genesis of a Program: Management Education for Nonprofit Organizations." In M. O'Neill and D.R. Young (eds.), *Educating Managers of Nonprofit Organizations*. New York: Praeger.

Keeton, M.T., and P.J. Tate (eds.). 1978. *Learning by Experience—What, Why, How*. New Directions for Experiential Learning, Number 1. San Francisco: Jossey-Bass.

Kettl, D. 1988. *Government by Proxy: (Mis?)Managing Federal Programs*. Washington: Congressional Quarterly Press.

Koziol, K. 1997. "Nonprofit Certificate Programs." Unpublished report. San Francisco: Institute for Nonprofit Organization Management, University of San Francisco.

Kymlicka, W., and W. Norman. 1994. "Return of the Citizen: A Survey of Recent Work on Citizenship Theory." *Ethics* 104 (January):352–381.

Lawson, H.A. 1990. "Beyond Positivism: Research, Practice, and Undergraduate Professional Education." *Quest* 42:161–183.

Leduc, R.F., and T.W. McAdam. 1988. "The Development of Useful Curricula for Nonprofit Management." In M. O'Neill and D.R. Young (eds.), *Educating Managers of Nonprofit Organizations*. New York: Praeger.

Levine, A. 1978. *Handbook on Undergraduate Curriculum*. San Francisco: Jossey-Bass.

Levy, D.C. 1986. *Private Education: Studies in Choice and Public Policy*. New York: Oxford University Press.

Lohmann, R. 1989. "And Lettuce Is Non Animal: Towards a Positive Economy of Voluntary Action." *Nonprofit and Voluntary Sector Quarterly* 18 (4):367–383.

Long, N.E. 1958. "The Local Community as an Ecology of Games." *American Journal of Sociology* 64 (3):251–261.

Lyons, M. 1994. *Australia's Nonprofit Sector*. 2nd ed. Centre for Community Organisations and Management. Working Paper No. 13. Sydney: University of Technology, CACOM.

Lyons, M. 1996. *Nonprofit Sector or Civil Society: Are They Competing Paradigms?* Centre for Community Organisations and Management Working Paper No. 35. Sydney: University of Technology, CACOM.

Maital, S. and S.L. Maital. 1984. *Economic Games People Play*. New York: Basic Books.

Marshall, T.H. 1965. "Citizenship and Social Class." Reprinted in T.H. Marshall, *Class, Citizenship, and Social Development*. New York: Anchor.

Mason, D.E. 1984. *Voluntary Nonprofit Enterprise Management*. New York: Plenum Press.

McCurley, S., and R. Lynch. 1989. *Essential Volunteer Management*. Downers Grove, IL: VMSystems and Heritage Arts Publishing.

McMillan, J. 1992. *Games, Strategies, and Managers*. New York: Oxford University Press.

Menzel, D.C. 1997. "Teaching Ethics and Values in Public Administration: Are We Making a Difference?" *Public Administration Review* 57 (3):224–231.

Milofsky, C. 1996. "The End of Nonprofit Management Education?" *Nonprofit and Voluntary Sector Quarterly* 25 (3):277–282.

Mintzberg, H. 1987. "Crafting Strategy." *Harvard Business Review* (July–August) 87 (4):66–77.

Monson, C.H. 1967. "Metaphors for the University." *Educational Record* 48:22–29.

Moore, J. 1995. "Fundraising by Computer: The Next Frontier?" *Chronicle of Philanthropy*, 7 (6):1, 22–24.

Murray, V., and B. Tassie, 1994. "Evaluating the Effectiveness of Nonprofit Organizations." In R.D. Herman and Associates (eds.), *The Jossey-Bass Handbook of Nonprofit Leadership and Management*. San Francisco: Jossey-Bass.

Muzzio, D. 1982. *Watergate Games*. New York: New York University Press.

National Association of Schools of Public Affairs and Administration. 1992. "Guidelines for Local Government Management Education." Report of the NASPAA/ICMA Task Force on Local Government Education. Washington, DC: NASPAA.

Nielsen, W. 1979. *The Endangered Sector*. New York: Columbia University Press.

Non-Profit Program, 1992. Simon Fraser University. "Educational Needs and Activities in the Voluntary Sector: An Exploratory Report on Learning Issues." Prepared for the B.C. Human Resource Development Project.

O'Connell, B. 1981. *Effective Leadership in Voluntary Organizations.* New York: Walker and Company.

O'Neill, M. 1989. *The Third America: The Emergence of the Nonprofit Sector in the United States.* San Francisco: Jossey-Bass.

O'Neill, M. 1990. "Ethical Dimensions of Nonprofit Administration." *Nonprofit Management and Leadership* 3 (2):199–213.

O'Neill, M. 1994. "Philanthropic Dimensions of Mutual Benefit Organizations." *Nonprofit and Voluntary Sector Quarterly* 23 (1):3–20.

O'Neill, M., and D.R. Young (eds.). 1988. *Educating Managers of Nonprofit Organizations.* New York: Praeger.

O'Regan, A., G. Donnelly-Cox, and G. MacKechnie. 1997. "Towards a Framework for the Investigation of Managerial Issues in the Irish Voluntary Sector." Paper presented to the Voluntary Action in Ireland, North and South Research Symposium, May 16, Trinity College, Dublin, Ireland.

Odendahl, T., and M. O'Neill. 1994. *Women and Power in the Nonprofit Sector.* San Francisco: Jossey-Bass.

Olshfski, D. 1994. "Teaching Public Administration by Exploiting Managerial Experience." *PS: Political Science and Politics* 27 (1):67–71.

Olson, M. 1965. *The Logic of Collective Action.* Cambridge: Harvard University Press.

Osborne, D., and T. Gaebler. 1992. *Reinventing Government: How the Entrepreneurial Spirit Is Transforming the Public Sector.* Reading, MA: Addison-Wesley.

Osborne, S.P., and M. Tricker. 1995. "Researching Nonprofit Organizational Effectiveness: A Comment on Herman and Heimovics." *Voluntas* 6 (1):85–92.

Oster, S.M. 1995. *Strategic Management for Nonprofit Organizations: Theory and Cases.* New York: Oxford University Press.

Ostrom, V. 1989. *The Intellectual Crisis in American Public Administration.* 2nd ed. Tuscaloosa: University of Alabama Press.

Owen, David. 1964. *English Philanthropy, 1600–1960.* Cambridge: Harvard University Press.

Paton, R. 1995. "How Are Values Handled in Voluntary Agencies?" In D. Billis and M. Harris (eds.), *Managing Voluntary Agencies.* London: Routledge.

Paton, R. 1996. "What's Different about Non-Profit and Voluntary Sector Marketing?— A Research Agenda." *Journal of Nonprofit and Voluntary Sector Marketing* 1 (1):23–31.

Paton, R., and C. Hooker. 1990. *Developing Managers in Voluntary Organisations: A Handbook.* Sheffield, England: Employment Department of Her Majesty's Government of the United Kingdom of Great Britain and Northern Ireland.

Patterson, S., and E.M. Vitello. 1994. "The Relationship between Credentialing and Professionalism: Adversarial or Synchronistic?" *Journal of Health Education* 25:201–203.

Pearce, J.L. 1993. *Volunteers: The Organizational Behavior of Unpaid Workers.* London: Routledge.

Project on Redefining the Meaning and Purpose of Baccalaureate Degrees. 1985. *Integrity in the College Curriculum: A Report to the Academic Community: The Findings and Recommendations of the Project on Redefining the Meaning and Purpose of Baccalaureate Degrees.* Washington, DC: Association of American Colleges.

Rubin, H., L. Adamski, and S.R. Block. 1989. "Toward a Discipline of Nonprofit Administration: Report from the Clarion Conference." *Nonprofit and Voluntary Sector Quarterly* 18 (3):279–286.

Ruddle, H., and F. Donoghue. 1995. *The Organization of Volunteering: A Study of Irish Voluntary Organizations in the Social Welfare Area.* Dublin, Ireland: Policy Research Center.

Salamon, L.M. 1981. "Rethinking Public Management: Third-Party Government and the Tools of Government Action." *Public Policy* 29:255–275.

Salamon, L.M. 1989. *Beyond Privatization: The Tools of Government Action.* Washington: Urban Institute Press.

Salamon, L.M. 1992. *America's Nonprofit Sector: A Primer.* New York: Foundation Center.

Salamon, L.M. 1995. *Partners in Public Service: Government-Nonprofit Relations in the Modern Welfare State.* Baltimore: Johns Hopkins University Press.

Salamon, L.M., and H.K. Anheier. 1998. "The Third Route: Social Service Provision in the United States and Germany." In W. Powell and E. Clemens (eds.), *Public Goods and Private Action.* New Haven: Yale University Press.

Scheier, I. 1997. Interview by Gretchen E. Stringer with Ivan Scheier, President of the Center for Creative Community, Santa Fe, New Mexico, August 7.

Schon, D. 1984. *The Reflective Practitioner: How Professionals Think in Action.* New York: Basic Books.

Seidman, H. 1986. *Politics, Position, and Power: The Politics of Government Organization.* 4th ed. New York: Oxford University Press.

Senge, P. 1990. "The Leader's New Work: Building Learning Organizations." *Sloan Management Review* 32 (1):7–23.

Silver, N. 1988. *At the Heart: The New Volunteer Challenge for Community Agencies.* San Francisco: San Francisco Foundation.

Simmons, K., and K. Szabat. 1996a. "Bridging the Scholar/Practitioner Gap." Philadelphia: LaSalle University, Nonprofit Management Development Center.

Simmons, K., and K. Szabat. 1996b. *Survey and Analysis of Management Support Organizations, 1994–1995.* Philadelphia: LaSalle University, Nonprofit Management Development Center.

Skelly, D.F. 1994. "Tax-Based Research and Data on Non-Profit Organizations." *Voluntas* 4 (4):555–568.

Slavin, S. 1988. "Different Types of Nonprofit Managers." In M. O'Neill and D.R. Young (eds.), *Educating Managers of Nonprofit Organizations.* New York: Praeger.

Smith, D.H. 1993. "Public Benefit and Member Benefit Nonprofit Voluntary Groups." *Nonprofit and Voluntary Sector Quarterly* 22 (1):53–68.

Smith, D.H. 1997. "The Rest of the Nonprofit Sector: Grassroots Associations as the Dark Matter Ignored in Prevailing 'Flat Earth' Maps of the Sector." *Nonprofit and Voluntary Sector Quarterly* 26 (2):114–131.

Steinberg, R. 1993. "Public Policy and the Performance of Nonprofit Organizations: A General Framework." *Nonprofit and Voluntary Sector Quarterly* 22 (1):13–32.

Stringer, G.E. 1993. "Report from the AVA Subcommittee on Volunteer Administration in Higher Education." *Journal of Volunteer Administration* 11 (3):5–12.

U.S. Internal Revenue Service. 1996. *Annual Report: Commissioner of Internal Revenue.* Washington, DC: Internal Revenue Service.

Van Til, J., and G. Hegyesi. 1996. "Education and Training in Nonprofit Management: An Interim Report of an International Study." Presented at University of San Francisco conference on "Nonprofit Management Education 1996: A U.S. and World Perspective," Berkeley, California.

Weisbrod, B.A. 1988. *The Nonprofit Economy.* Cambridge: Harvard University Press.

Whetten, D.A. and K.S. Cameron. 1991. *Developing Management Skills.* New York: HarperCollins.

Whitehead, J.S. 1973. *The Separation of College and State: Columbia, Dartmouth, Harvard, and Yale, 1776–1876.* New Haven: Yale University Press.

Winter Commission. 1993. "Hard Truths/Tough Choices: An Agenda for State and Local Reform." In F. J. Thompson (ed.), *Revitalizing State and Local Public Service.* San Francisco: Jossey-Bass.

Wish, N.B. 1991. "University- and College-Based Nonprofit Management Programs in the United States." Washington, DC: National Association of Schools of Public Affairs and Administration.

Wish, N.B. 1993. "Graduate Programs in Nonprofit Management: An Update." *Journal of the National Association of Graduate Admissions Professionals* 5 (2):15–20.

Wood, M. 1992. "Is Governing Board Behavior Cyclical?" *Nonprofit Management and Leadership* 3 (2):139–163.

Index

About the Editors and Contributors

JULIAN BATSLEER is Lecturer in Management Development and Director, Certificate and Diploma Programmes, Open University Business School, England. He helped to develop the curriculum of the university's Voluntary Sector Management Programme. His research interests include organizational development and management education.

JEFFREY L. BRUDNEY is Professor of Political Science and Director, Doctor of Public Administration Program, University of Georgia. His publications include studies of volunteer administration, public administration, and applied statistics. He has chaired the Section on Public Administration of the American Political Science Association and the Section on Public Administration Education of the American Society for Public Administration.

CHRIS CORNFORTH is Senior Lecturer and Head of the Centre for Comparative Management in the Open University Business School, England. He is co-founder of the university's Voluntary Sector Management Programme. His most recent research project focuses on the governance of nonprofit organizations.

NORMAN A. DOLCH is Professor of Sociology, Department of Social Sciences, Louisiana State University in Shreveport. His research interests include family medicine and comprehensive care, community groups, race, and community studies.

GEMMA DONNELLY-COX is Lecturer in Business Studies in the School of Business Studies, Trinity College, Dublin, Ireland. She is co-founder of the Voluntary Organization Research Group at Trinity College. Her research interests include institutional approaches to organizational change and innovation, public sector change management, and the use of metaphor in organization theory.

KATHLEEN FLETCHER is a consultant and researcher in nonprofit management, a doctoral student in the School of Education at the University of San Francisco, and an instructor and former staff member of the university's Institute for Nonprofit Organization Management. Her research interests include nonprofit boards, strategic planning, and fundraising.

ROLAND KIDWELL, JR. is Assistant Professor, Department of Commerce, Niagara University. His research interests include collective action in organizational contexts, strategic human resource management, electronic monitoring and surveillance, and small business management.

MARK LYONS is Associate Professor, School of Management, University of Technology, Sydney, Australia, and former Director of the Australian Council of Social Service. He is the founder and director of the nonprofit management education program at the University of Technology, Sydney. His research interests include the Australian nonprofit sector, theories of nonprofit activity, and the privatization of human services.

GEOFFREY MACKECHNIE is Senior Lecturer in Organizational Behavior in the School of Business Studies, Trinity College, Dublin, Ireland. He is Head of the School of Business Studies and co-founder of the Voluntary Organization Research Group in Trinity College. His primary research interest is organization design. Recent publications include work on organizational networks, public sector management, and managing professionals in complex organizations.

ROSEANNE M. MIRABELLA is Assistant Professor, Graduate Department of Public Administration, Seton Hall University, and teaches and advises in the university's MPA concentration in nonprofit management. She is Director of the Nonprofit Sector Resource Institute of New Jersey and Co-Director of the Institute for Service Learning. Her research interests include public administration and organization theory, public policy analysis, and management and human resources.

MICHAEL O'NEILL is Professor in the Department of Public Management and Director of the Institute for Nonprofit Organization Management, College of Professional Studies, University of San Francisco. He is the President of the Association for Research on Nonprofit Organizations and Voluntary Action. His research interests include the American nonprofit sector, mutual benefit organizations, ethics and diversity in the nonprofit sector, and nonprofit management education.

ROB PATON is Senior Lecturer in Management in the Open University Business School, England. He directed the university's Voluntary Sector Management Programme from 1988 to 1994. His research interests include the management of voluntary organizations, worker cooperatives, management development, and the rhetoric of management.

JEFFREY SADOW is Associate Professor of Political Science, Louisiana State University in Shreveport. His research interests include American political behavior, political theory, and international relations.

LESTER M. SALAMON is Professor, Johns Hopkins University, and Director of the Johns Hopkins Center for Civil Society Studies. His publications include studies of the federal government budget and the nonprofit sector, the international dimensions of nonprofit activity, theories of the nonprofit sector, and social welfare policy.

JIMMIE SMITH is Professor and Chair, Department of Psychology, Louisiana State University in Shreveport, where he has been President of the Faculty Senate, Vice Chancellor for Student Affairs, and Director of Student Development. His research interests include race, gender, learning disabilities, and self-esteem.

RICK SMITH is Vice President for Operations at Strategic Marketing Resources in San Leandro, California. He is former National Executive Director of the Support Centers of America and former Executive Director of the Support Center for Nonprofit Management in San Francisco. He is an adjunct faculty member at the University of California at Berkeley and Golden Gate University in San Francisco.

GRETCHEN E. STRINGER is Instructor at the Empire State College and Niagara Community College. She is Partner and Managing Officer of the NonProfit Management Center located at Houghton College in West Seneca, New York. For more than 20 years she has been a trainer and consultant in volunteer administration and is an active board member and volunteer in nonprofit organizations.

MARY TSCHIRHART is Assistant Professor, Policy and Administration Faculty Group, School of Public and Environmental Affairs, Indiana University at Bloomington. She led the development of the nonprofit management graduate concentration on the Bloomington campus and the nonprofit management certificate for all Indiana University campuses. Her research interests include organizational behavior, human resource management, and volunteerism.

NAOMI B. WISH is Professor, Director of the Center for Public Service, and Chair of the Graduate Department of Public Administration at Seton Hall University. She developed New Jersey's only MPA concentration and graduate certificate program in nonprofit management. She has published several articles on university-based nonprofit management programs in the United States and was the Chair of the Nonprofit Management Education Section of the National Association of Schools of Public Affairs and Administration.

DENNIS R. YOUNG is Professor of Nonprofit Management and Economics at Case Western Reserve University. He is the former Director of the Mandel Center for Nonprofit Organizations at Case Western and developed a nonprofit concentration while Professor at the Harriman School, State University of New York at Stony

Brook. He is the founder and editor of *Nonprofit Management and Leadership* and the President-Elect of the Association for Research on Nonprofit Organizations and Voluntary Action.

ISBN 0-275-96115-X

HARDCOVER BAR CODE